Who wanted war?

The origin of the war according to diplomatic documents

by

ÉMILE DURKHEIM and ERNEST DENIS

Translated by A. M. WILSON-GARINÉI

QUID PRO BOOKS
New Orleans, Louisiana

WHO WANTED WAR?

Originally published in 1915 by Librarie Armand Colin, Paris, France (in an English language edition, translated from the original 1915 French edition). No copyright is claimed in the original text; or in any quoted material, texts, or excerpts therein; or in photography. This is an unabridged edition.

Published in 2012 by Quid Pro Books.

ISBN 978-1-61027-148-6 (pbk.)
ISBN 978-1-61027-149-3 (eBook)

QUID PRO BOOKS
Quid Pro, LLC
5860 Citrus Blvd., Suite D-101
New Orleans, Louisiana 70123
www.quidprobooks.com

CONTENTS

Page numbers in brackets below reference the original pagination of the 1915 printing in translation. Page numbers shown to the right below (and without brackets) refer to the current pagination of this edition.

INTRODUCTION: NOTES OF THE EDITOR

As the contemporary editor at Quid Pro Books for this classic monograph, I have tried as much as possible to recreate *Who Wanted War?* as Émile Durkheim and Ernest Denis intended it in 1915 and as Librarie Armand Colin of Paris, France, published it that year in translation. Other recent reproductions of this classic book, when compared to the original source, all failed to produce it accurately—especially the digital versions available. I sincerely doubt that Durkheim and Denis originally wrote, "/.–The Australian Ultimatum and Servians Reply. (July 23rd-25'ft) On the a8 th of June 191^,at Sarajevo...," or intended that their meticulous footnotes be blended into text without indication. The authors and this important work of world and diplomatic history simply deserve better.

Such respect is especially owed to these important and careful writers. Émile Durkheim (1858-1917), who died just two years after the publication of this book, is considered the founding father of the discipline of sociology and had long been, by then, a world-renowned scholar. He remains much studied today on matters of social history, theory, labor, and religion. Ernest Denis (1849-1921), who himself died soon after—but not before having major influence in the post-war Europe—was a history professor and Durkheim's respected colleague at the University of Paris. Denis specialized in Slavic and German history and is considered to be a very influential figure in the establishment of the Czechoslovak state in 1918. The book was part of the French series *Studies and Documents on the War*, whose list of participants is retained from the original printing.

The care required in republishing this work for today's reader is especially crucial given that it originated in a book translated and published very quickly in its time, in order to have the influential effect intended throughout the world in the midst of World War I. (Indeed, the book reads nearly like a summary of current events in its day, in the second year of the Great War, and certainly preceded American entry into the war in 1917.) The original printing was in fact missing occasional letters and even some words. And it was arranged in what may be considered an understandably hurried fashion (e.g., indicating footnotes by a number in parenthesis rather than a superscript, and many commas instead printed as periods).

To restore it to its obvious intent and to make the arrangement usable to modern readers—to remaster it, if you will—required more than just a mechanical reproduction, and particularly in digital formats simply does not always make sense as literally appearing on the page.

Even so, I have made no attempt to make substantive editorial changes to the book—except to recreate, as much as possible, the intended prose and punctuation of the original monograph, while making it accessible to current researchers and readers. The editorial license occasionally taken is detailed in further notes below.

On a substantive note, the book had obvious propaganda purposes, and is to some extent (perhaps to a large extent) a partisan rendition of facts. But the authors carried with them a worldwide credibility and pressed their case, in this "brief" if you will, in such a meticulous and supported way that their conclusions seem reasonable. There is no particular reason to question the actual summary of facts. These remain useful to historians and those curious about more than the usual recitation of the causes behind World War I.

Nevertheless, the modern reader may want to reconsider some of the conclusions and assignment of responsibility offered by the authors, using the 20-20 hindsight that is so readily available not only after the Great War but also after World War II. In particular, even accepting the rendition of facts as neutral, one might question whether leaders of Great Britain did all they could to dissuade German expansion of the conflict. Some of the quotes these authors share from English sources, though interpreted here as a warning that England would not make a side deal with Germany and made strong statements of protestation to that effect, perhaps were read by the German recipients as a lack of resolve against them—or even, in modern terms, an invitation to "appeasement."

Is it possible that Sir Edward Grey's stern commitment to keep all options open (in his role as Britain's Foreign Secretary at the time) may have also contributed to a sense in Berlin that Britain would not enter the war against them even if it would not support them? Might not a sterner statement that German aggression would indeed force English involvement in favor of the Allies have given more pause in Germany than the less committal warnings cataloged so carefully here? One wonders whether, among other themes that can be teased out from this narrative, might be the failure of diplomacy and resolve in other quarters than the authors point to.

In any event, there is no doubt that much material is here worth considering by a new generation of historians, at least for the facts pieced together so carefully, and even for the advocates' presentation of them. It deserves to remain part of the essential literature on the war and on the breakdown of diplomacy—so much richer than the usual litany that an assassination in Sarajevo simply triggered complex, pre-existing alliances into a pan-European War.

Moreover, the timeline and diplomatic near-misses so vividly set out here (some apparently unnoticed by the authors themselves) are as compelling as watching a train wreck. Readers may find themselves inexplicably hopeful at certain developments—all while well aware, a century or so after, of the tragic denouement.

We thus determined that the book deserved a modern and clean new presentation. Even a close proofreading of the original materials was in order.

Although it is inevitable that some errors will creep into a reproduction of an earlier work converted into modern print and ebook formats, we have sought to minimize these and to respect the authors and their work. Such pervasive errors and deletions as noted above, and the decision to interlace footnote entries into the work without informing the reader adequately, distract from the care and depth of this meticulous work. A republication's presentation should not misstate the authors' intent, nor make it difficult to understand.

Thus, the principal goal of this new edition was to convey the essential meaning of the authors, so far as possible in their own words (at least as presented in the original 1915 translation by A. M. Wilson-Garinéi, a Cambridge student who died—in the war?—before his effort was published). We wanted it to be a fitting tribute to this important work. Yet it should speak to a new generation of students and readers with modern formatting and presentation that is accessible to them, and correct obvious but distracting printing errors in the text. We have emphasized accuracy of text and the authors' intent, proper contemporary formatting, and usefulness to new readers.

To that end, producing this classic work for a modern format, to include ebooks, required a few alterations that were necessary today, given the technology, even under the goal of carefully recreating Durkheim and Denis's work. Some notes to keep in mind:

- The numbering of the footnotes is consecutive throughout, unlike in the original 1915 edition. That used the older convention of renumbering from 1 (actually, from "I") at the beginning of each new page. This does not work for ebooks or endnotes, of course, and could not be replicated without confusing the reader with scores of footnote I's and 2's. Even so, it is possible for the reader to discern the original numbering for many of the notes, if necessary for purposes of citation or research, given the identity of the page numbers found in the Contents.
- The actual, original page numbers of section transitions are detailed in the original Contents page, which is retained here (and to some extent expanded). That page appeared at the back of the original, but is moved to the book's front matter in this edition, for accessibility and to lay out the organization and argument.
- We have made minor, consistent spacing changes through-

out for legibility, without changing the words or quotability in any way. For example, we delete extra space around punctuation such as quotation marks and semi-colons.

- The roman numeral I, when clearly intended to represent the arabic 1, is presented as a 1.
- Because the original footnote references in text were inserted at the end of sentences in parentheticals such as (3), we moved the now-superscripted number slightly to a more appropriate place, such as after the immediate punctuation instead of inside of it. We have otherwise retained the British order of punctuation used, such as having a period follow the quotation mark.
- In ebook formats, the footnotes are presented as endnotes, as of course they must be in the flowing digital format. Nevertheless, they are fully linked to allow ready reference to them (and back). The consecutive numeration follows that of this new paperback edition.
- Durkheim and Denis's prose is generally reproduced as Wilson-Garinéi presented it in English, without substantive editing. The book is an unabridged version of the original 1915 presentation. But in several passages where there was an obvious misprint (e.g., a word printed twice, the wrong word printed, a missing closing quote mark, misnumbered footnotes), we have taken the liberty of correcting the error. We have kept such changes to a minimum and only when it is clear that the wrong word was printed or the like.
- We have not updated anachronistic spellings such as to-day, skilful and Servia. But we have corrected clear misspellings (or misprintings) when considered from the perspective of the time, or inconsistent with their appearance elsewhere in the book (e.g., safenguard, governement).
- We have made consistent some minor formatting choices in the original, such as the way chapter titles are presented (with or without a period).
- In one place, in a footnote, where the original printing simply was too compromised to fully reveal one phrase (which,

fortunately, does not seem to be necessary to understand the whole), we have indicated the printer's lapse with a bracketed {?}.

As noted, this edition was designed to include a digital platform, where the gap in availability is stark and the quality of available formats is particularly poor. The print edition and the various ebook versions are designed to be consistent among themselves, and to share continuity with earlier printings—all to make classroom assignment and referencing easier for teachers and scholars. Other classic works in history and the social sciences, in ebook and print formats, are available at multiple retail sites and at *www.quidprobooks.com.* These include two other books by Durkheim, as well as foundational works by Oliver Wendell Holmes, Jr., Talcott Parsons, Woodrow Wilson, John Chipman Gray, and Benjamin Cardozo. In addition, also about World War I, the publisher offers a first-hand contemporary account from a battlefield nurse, Shirley Millard's *I Saw Them Die*, which is extensively introduced by my Tulane colleague Elizabeth Townsend Gard.

STEVEN ALAN CHILDRESS
Conrad Meyer III Professor of Law,
Tulane University

New Orleans, Louisiana
October, 2012

PHOTOGRAPHS AND IMAGES

Émile Durkheim

Émile Durkheim

Sir Edward Grey, 1st Viscount Grey of Fallodon, 1914

William II (Wilhelm II) of Germany, left,
and Nicholas II of Russia, right, c. 1905

STUDIES AND DOCUMENTS ON THE WAR

Who wanted war?

The origin of the war according to diplomatic documents

by

É. DURKHEIM and E. DENIS

Professors at the University of Paris

Translated by

A. M. WILSON-GARINEI

Late student of Newnham College Cambridge,
Modern Languages Tripos.

Cette brochure est en vente à la

LIBRAIRIE ARMAND COLIN

103, Boulevard Saint-Michel, PARIS, 5•

au prix de 0 fr. 50

STUDIES AND DOCUMENTS ON THE WAR

PUBLISHING COMMITTEE

All communications to be addressed to the Secretary of the Committee:

M. ÉMILE DURKHEIM, 4, Avenue d'Orléans, PARIS, 14.

STUDIES AND DOCUMENTS ON THE WAR

Who wanted war?

The origin of the war according to diplomatic documents

LIBRAIRIE ARMAND COLIN

103, Boulevard Saint-Michel, PARIS, 5•

1915

WHO WANTED WAR?

Like all historical events, the present war depends, in some measure, on causes of a profound and remote nature. Historians will one day have to investigate the demographic, economic and ethnic conditions owing to which occasions for conflict seemed, for some time, to have been multiplying among the peoples; how the precarious state of the Austro-Hungarian Empire, the development of the Balkan peoples, the clearer self-consciousness to which certain nationalities were awakening, were bound, in a future more or less imminent, to determine the reconstruction of the map of Europe; finally, how from all this there resulted a feeling of unrest and anxiety which prepared the minds of men for war.

But whatever may be the importance of these impersonal causes, they cannot act by themselves; they can only produce their effect through the will of man. When war breaks out, it is because some State wishes for war and that State must bear the responsibility. If during the last ten years we passed through very serious crises — the Conference of Algeçiras, the affairs of Casablanca and of Agadir, the annexation of Bosnia and Herzegovina, the Balkan Wars — and no European war resulted from them, it was not because the moral situation of Europe was more satisfactory than it is to-day, but because men desirous of peace succeeded in averting the danger. If this time the catastrophe has taken place, it means that these men, or certain among them, have changed their opinion. And therefore the question presents itself: where has this change been produced? Which nation wished for war in preference to peace and what was its reason for preferring it?

It is this question that we propose to discuss. It forces itself so naturally upon our attention that each of us has, most likely, already answered it in his own way. But until lately it was difficult for us to have on this point an enlightened and well thoughtout opinion; our information was too fragmentary to enable us to view the crisis as a whole, and to follow it during the course of its development. To-day we have at our disposal several collections of diplomatic documents which, emanating from different governments, complete and mutually check one another.[1] Though they probably do not reveal all the secrets of the chancelleries yet they permit us at least to trace, step by step, the series of negotiations which took place during that week of terrible suspense when the fate of Europe was at stake. We can now distinguish the successive periods and enquire at each stage; what was done for peace and what against it, whence came the attempts at conciliation and whence a tacit or avowed resistance. Our inventory made, we can establish the moral balance-sheet of the different actors in the drama and thus determine the share of responsibility that falls to each of them. Such is the object and such is the plan of the study we are about to make.

This study is all the more necessary as the German Government has already taken up the question and has professed to solve it by means of documents exclusively German. The solution which the German Government gives of it is set forth in the Preface to the *White Book;* according to it, Russia is responsible for the war. We cannot leave unanswered an allegation which has been so widely circulated. Yet, though we feel we ought to mention it at the very beginning of this work, we do not intend to take it expressly to task nor to discuss it in itself.

---

[1] We have five collections of this kind: the Russian book known as the *Orange Book* (*O. B.),* the French book or *Yellow Book (Y. B.),* the Belgian book or *Grey Book (G. B.),* the German book or *White Book (W. B.)* and the book published by the British Government under the title *Correspondence respecting the European Crisis (B. Cor.).* When our work was in the press the Servian book appeared but it adds nothing of importance to the preceding.

To prove its worth, it is sufficient to state the facts simply and honestly in the order that they come, contenting ourselves with pointing out on the way, what these facts have become in the German reading of them. Once these statements are given – reference to them will be found in the foot-notes[2] – the conclusion will be evident in itself.

But whilst entering upon the subject of this work, we must not forget that we ourselves are judge and a party in the debate since our own country is concerned. We, and our leaders in particular, must therefore be on guard against the possible influence of a national partiality, however natural it may be. For that reason we shall restrict ourselves to giving first a complete and objective account of events, without making any comment. We shall then allow ourselves to draw our conclusions, but by that time it will be easy for the reader to check, by the narrative which has gone before, the result at which we shall have arrived.

---

[2] To draw the reader's attention to these notes we have printed them in italics.

I. — The Austrian Ultimatum and Servia's Reply (July 23rd–25th).

On the 28th of June 1914, at Serajevo, the administrative capital of Bosnia, the Archduke Francis Ferdinand, the heir presumptive to the throne of Austria-Hungary and his wife the Duchess of Hohenberg, were assassinated. This double crime was the starting-point of the war.

The assassins were manifestly conspirators who wished to protest by this act against the annexation of Bosnia and Herzegovina by Austria, and to prepare the way for the reunion of these provinces with Servia. For this reason Austria at once declared it to be evident, that the origin of this plot must be sought in Belgrade, and that it had been organised, if not by the Servian Government, at least by societies which the Government had wrongfully tolerated and even protected. The enquiry ordered by the Austrian Government was conducted in this spirit and it was easy to foretell the result. Scarcely had it begun when the unofficial press announced that "steps" of a threatening character were about to be taken to force Servia to cease its criminal machinations. Already on the 2nd of July the French Ambassador, M. Dumaine, warned his Government that the situation gave him cause for anxiety.[3] But as if by word of command, when the moment approached for the result of the enquiry to be published, the tone changed. Instead of "steps are about to be taken" we find "negotiations are about to take place". Count Tisza made a speech in the Austrian Parliament, the moderation of which went so far as to exasperate certain newspapers.[4] Optimism became the leading note in the official press. On the 23rd of July Baron Macchio, general secretary of

---

3 *Y. B.*, no 8.

4 *Y. B.*, nos 11 and 12.

the Austrian Foreign Office, again assured M. Dumaine that "a pacific conclusion could be counted on".[5]

On that very day Austria had her Ultimatum sent to Belgrade.

The bellicose nature of the Austrian Ultimatum. – This ultimatum is so well known that it is not necessary to reproduce it here; we shall merely recall to the reader's mind its essential articles.

The Austrian Government, considering as an established fact that the Serajevo assassinations had been planned in Belgrade, demanded that the Servian Government should take certain measures to prevent a repetition of similar outrages.

First of all the Servian Government was to publish a declaration on the first page of the *Official Journal* of the 26th July, the form of which was strictly dictated, by which it condemned all propaganda against Austria-Hungary, expressed its regrets that public officials should have participated in such propaganda and promised henceforward to punish severely all persons found guilty of similar acts. This declaration was also to be communicated to the army.

Moreover it had to pledge itself:

1. To suppress any publication directed against Austria.

2. To dissolve the society styled Narodna Odbrana, accused in particular of engaging in active propaganda against the Austro-Hungarian Monarchy, to confiscate its means of action and to proceed in the same manner against all societies which might be formed in future for similar purposes.

3. To eliminate from the state schools all persons and all methods of instruction that might facilitate the abovementioned propaganda.

4. To remove from the army and from the administration all those officers and officials whom the Austrian Government should indicate as being guilty in this way.

---

5 *Y. B.*, no 20.

5. To accept the collaboration of representatives of the Royal and Imperial Government in the "suppression" of this subversive movement.

6. To take judicial proceedings against accessories to the Serajevo plot in Servian territory; "delegates of the Austro-Hungarian Government will take part in the investigation relating thereto".

7. To proceed without delay to the arrest of two Servian subjects accused in particular of being implicated in the plot.

8. To prevent the illicit traffic in arms and explosives across the frontier and to punish the officials who had permitted or facilitated such traffic.

9. To furnish the Dual Monarchy with explanations regarding the hostile utterances of high Servian officials both in Servia and abroad.

10. To notify the Austrian Government of the execution of the measures above-mentioned.

Servia was given forty-eight hours in which to make known her reply.

No sooner had the ultimatum been published, than the unanimous opinion of the chancelleries was that it had been conceived and drawn up "so as to render war inevitable". Sir M. de Bunsen, English Ambassador at Vienna says: "I have had conversations with all my colleagues representing the Great Powers. The impression left on my mind is . . . that the Austro-Hungarian Government is fully resolved to have war with Servia".[6] The Austrian demands were in fact of such a kind that no State could submit to them without sacrificing its entire independence. Not only was Servia deeply humiliated by having to make a public apology in terms which she was not even allowed to discuss, but further, her sovereignty was infringed by the intervention of foreign officials in a judicial enquiry and in her administrative action; she was treated as the vassal of Austria. The very tone of the note seemed intended to offend the State to which it was addressed and thus to make

[6] *B. Cor.*, no 41.

submission more difficult. What could be more offensive than the brevity of the delay granted Servia for reflexion? It was to lay down as a principle that the result of the Austrian enquiry although that enquiry had been one-sided and singularly summary, allowed of no discussion.[7]

Moreover, the date chosen, the proceedings adopted, everything tended to prove that the object was to prevent any intervention in favour of peace. The optimism professed by the Austrian official papers at the last moment, and which events were so soon to belie, had managed to lull the mistrust even of those States most interested in following the matter closely. The Russian Ambassador at Vienna had just gone on leave, after receiving formal assurances that all would be well.[8] President Poincaré, accompanied by M. Viviani, Minister for Foreign Affairs, was visiting the northern capitals.[9] The French Minister was absent from Belgrade on account of illness. The diplomatists of the Triple Entente could not therefore easily take concerted action in order to intervene between the two adversaries. Besides, they were not given the time. The Ultimatum was not communicated to the Powers until the 24th of July, the day after it had been sent to Belgrade. They therefore had little more than twenty-four hours in which to prevent the rupture.

This bellicose attitude was, moreover, acclaimed by a large section of public opinion. War was desired and the moment was judged favourable. "If we do not make up our minds to go to war now" wrote the *Militärische Rundschau*, "we shall have to do so in two or three years' time, and under much less favourable conditions. As we shall be obliged to accept the struggle one day, let us provoke it at once". And the *Neue Freie Presse* was indignant at the very thought of attempting a pacific arrangement. It considered that a peaceful settlement could

---

7 We leave entirely on one side the question of the value of Austria's allegations; they have too little influence on the course of events.

8 *Y. B.*, no 18.

9 *Y. B.*, no 25.

follow only "a *war to the knife* against pan-Serbism".[10] Thus, once the Ultimatum had been sent, the only fear was that Servia might yield.[11] On the 25th of July Sir M. Bunsen writes: "The language of the press leaves the impression that the surrender of Servia is neither expected nor really desired".[12]

Now war with Servia was the open door to a European war. It would certainly be unjust to say that everyone in Vienna had deliberately wished for this extension of the conflict. We are assured that Count Berchtold and his circle would have been content with "localised operations against Servia". But on the other hand a whole faction deemed it necessary "to make a move before Russia had completed the great improvements she was making in her army and her railways, and before France had brought her military organisation to perfection".[13] In any case, even the most moderate must have been aware that it might not be possible to limit the war area once war had broken out.

The Ultimatum was known to Germany. – Was the heavy responsibility thus assumed by Austria shared by Germany? Did she know of the ultimatum before its publication, and did she encourage her ally to run the risk?

The Chancellor, Herr von Bethmann-Hollweg, and the Secretary of State for Foreign Affairs, Herr von Jagow, have always maintained that they were totally ignorant of the Austrian demands before they were communicated to Belgrade, and that if they approved of them without reserve, yet they could not be held responsible for them.

But these repeated affirmations were generally looked on with scepticism and unbelief. It seemed incredible that Germany could support the Austrian pretensions and with what

---

[10] *Y. B.*, no 12.

[11] *Y. B.*, no 27.

[12] *B. Cor.*, no 20.

[13] *Y. B.*, no 14.

energy we shall see, if she had been ignorant of their import.[14] It seemed as improbable that Herr von Tschirsky, the German Ambassador at Vienna, already a party to violent resolutions, should have been held in ignorance of what was being schemed. In fact, Sir M. de Bunsen declares that he had "private information that *the German Ambassador knew the text of the Austrian ultimatum to Servia before it was despatched, and telegraphed it to the German Emperor*".[15]

Moreover we have to-day a whole collection of evidence which confirms this presumption.

There exists in Germany a measure preparatory to mobilisation, which consists in informing men and officers in the reserve to hold themselves ready in case of a speedy call to arms. This is according to M. Cambon, "a *general alert*" (un garde à vous général) which is resorted to in moments of tension. This notice had been issued in 1911 during the negotiations relative to Morocco.[16] Now, from the 21st of July, 1914, Mr Cambon was informed that this preliminary notice of mobilisation had been addressed "to the classes that should receive it in a similar case".[17] It was at this very moment that Austria set to work to reassure Europe. We must believe that Germany, too, was informed of what was in preparation.

At about the same time (23rd of July), the Bavarian Prime Minister, whilst discussing the Austro-Servian incident with our Minister at Munich, was led to say that he "had knowledge" of the Austrian note.[18] Now, at that date Servia had not yet received it, and it was only made known to the Powers on the 24th. How can we admit that Austria could have been silent to

---

14 *Y. B.*, no 30.

15 *B. Cor.*, no 95.

16 *Y. B.*, no 3.

17 *Y. B.*, no 15.

18 *Y. B.*, no 21.

Germany on what she had thought it her duty to confide to Bavaria?[19]

Besides we have the admission of the German Government itself. In the Preface to the *White Book*, after reviewing the situation in which Austria found herself, owing to the Serajevo outrage, the official writer adds: "Under these circumstances, Austria could not help but realise, that neither her dignity nor care for her safety would allow her to remain longer an inactive spectator of these machinations. *The Imperial and Royal Government made known to us its view of the matter and asked our opinion. From the bottom of our heart we were able to tell our ally that we agreed entirely with him in his way of viewing the situation, and to assure him that any action he should consider necessary, to put an end to the movement directed in Servia against the existence of the monarchy, would have our approbation.* By acting thus we were perfectly aware that Austria-Hungary's bellicose attitude towards Servia might cause Russia to enter the arena, and that we, conformably to our duties as ally, might be drawn ourselves into the war. *We therefore left Austria an absolutely free hand to act as she thought fit against Servia.* But we took no part in the way in which she organised this action".[20] This is an admission that Germany knew, if not the actual terms, at least the spirit of the ultimatum and its general contents. It is possible that she did not know the terms of the despatch in detail. But even if she knew as little as she alleged, that fact which is of very secondary interest, did not authorise the German Government to declare so positively that it knew no more of the Austrian Note than did the other Powers, and that it in no way shared in the responsibility. Whatever it may say it knew the essential part.

It not only knew it but it had approved of it. It agreed with it from the bottom of its heart, to borrow the expression

---

[19] The Bavarian Government thought fit later to deny this statement; but its author, M. Allizé, maintains it integrally. Perhaps the Bavarian Government plays on the words; it was ignorant of the text of the note, but certainly knew the contents.

[20] *W. B.*, Pref., p. 4-5.

above-quoted. It had made it its own. Germany must therefore be regarded as being co-partner with Austria in a step which the latter would never have dared to take, had she not been sure of the support of her powerful ally. Moreover public opinion in Berlin was as much inclined to war as was public opinion in Vienna. "All the newspapers", writes the Russian delegate at Berlin, on the 24th of July, "welcome with the greatest sympathy the energetic tone adopted by Austria, even those who recognise the impossibility of Servia's accepting the terms demanded".[21] M. Cambon says: "A person of importance in Germany told me confidentially that it was feared here that Servia might accept the entire Austrian note".[22] Germany herself had, from the beginning, a clearer consciousness of the risks to which she was exposing Europe; whereas in Austria it seems to have been thought that Russia would not "resist the blow" (ne tiendrait pas le coup) to quote the words of a diplomatist, and would leave matters alone.[23] On the contrary, on the 28th of July, in a confidential note, the German Chancellor warned the confederate Governments that if Russia intervened in favour of Servia, a European war would be the result.[24]

The Attitude of the Powers. The first attempts at conciliation repulsed by Germany and Austria. – From this moment Germany, although not directly interested in the question, comes to the front, and her attitude is distinctly uncompromising and even threatening.

On the 24th of July Herr von Schoen went to M. Bienvenu-Martin, temporary Minister for Foreign Affairs and stated the point of view of his Government Germany considers, said he, that the question concerns Austria and Servia alone; it should therefore be settled between those two countries. Any intervention by another Power would have "incalculable con-

---

[21] *O. B.*, no 7.

[22] *Y. B.*, no 47.

[23] *Y. B.*, nos 12 and 50; *B. Cor.*, nos 71 and 80.

[24] *W. B.*, no 2.

sequences by bringing the alliances into play".[25] This was equivalent to refusing to Russia the right of intervention.[26] Now every one knew very well that it was morally and politically impossible for Russia to stand completely aside. There exist close bonds of sympathy between the Russian people and the Servian nation, arising not only from a community of historical traditions but also from a feeling of racial brotherhood. The great Russia, the natural and traditional protector of Slav communities, could not leave little Servia defenceless. Besides Russia herself had vital interests at stake; for Servia, once vanquished, would become an Austrian vassal, and that would mean the equilibrium of the Balkans upset for the profit of Austria".[27] Servia dominated by Austria", said one day M. Sazonoff, Russian Minister for Foreign Affairs, "is as intolerable to Russia as the domination of the Netherlands by Germany would be to Great Britain. It is for Russia a question of life or death".[28] Beyond Servia therefore, Russia was aimed at and attacked by the ultimatum and the question as put by Germany might be expressed thus: either the weakening of Russia's prestige and her humiliation, or war.

The other Powers were unanimous in seeing in the ultimatum a scandal both in international law and in diplomacy. Sir E. Grey says, "I have never before seen one State address to another independent State a document of so formidable a character".[29] Italy herself, though she was the ally of Austria

---

[25] *Y. B.*, no 28.

[26] The next day, it is true, Herr von Schoen protested that there was nothing of a threatening nature in his communication (*Y. B.*, no 36). The same day, in London, the Austrian Ambassador explained to Sir E. Grey that the Austrian note was not an ultimatum but "a démarche with a time limit" (*Cor. B.*, no 14) and that is was merely a question of "military preparations, not of operations". These verbal protestations, which events were to belie, were only a means for allaying anxiety and for keeping back the activity of the Powers.

[27] *B. Cor.*, no 97.

[28] *B. Cor.*, no 139.

[29] *B. Cor.*, no 5.

and Germany, made it known "that she would probably not have approved of the Austrian note", had it been communicated to her before its publication, and she declined "all responsibility in the grave initiative taken by Austria".[30] Under these conditions, had Russia really wished for war as Germany has since accused her of doing, it was easy for her to attain her aim; she had only to let events follow their course. On the contrary, M. Sazonoff immediately announced that he was resolved to try every means to stop the conflict. He said to M. Paléologue, the French Ambassador at St. Petersburg: "We must avoid everything which might precipitate the crisis. I consider that even if the Austro-Hungarian Government should proceed to action against Servia, we ought not to break off negotiations".[31] He acted as he spoke and not only France but England and Italy joined him in his efforts.

Germany, by her Ambassador in London, had from the outset asked England to exert her influence at St. Petersburg by advising non-intervention, in other words, by defending there the German point of view. Sir E. Grey replied that the terms of the ultimatum did not justify him in doing so, for the Russian Government had good grounds for considering the Austrian demands inadmissible.[32] But he proposed that the great Powers should together exercise a moderating influence at Vienna and St. Petersburg. For that purpose, German co-operation was naturally indispensable. It was asked but categorically refused. The German Government replied that it could not "interfere in

---

[30] *Y. B.*, no 56.

[31] *Y. B.*, no 38.

[32] Yet we read in the Preface to the *White Book*, that "both the French and English Governments had promised to act with the German Government" (p. 6). We are taken aback at seeing a statement, manifestly contrary to the truth, made so cooly. England and France would never have assented to leaving Russia aside.

the conflict".[33] Thus the attempts made to find a way of conciliation came to nothing.[34]

Henceforward negotiations became difficult. As the time limit granted by the ultimatum was very short, it was judged most urgent to obtain an extension. In this way there would be time to take counsel before an irreparable act had been committed. The proposal was made by M. Sazonoff;[35] France, England and Italy promised to support it.[36] It could, moreover, easily be justified; time was necessary for the Powers to examine Austria's grievances. The request was addressed simultaneously to Berlin and to Vienna. In Berlin, when the Russian chargé d'affaires, M. Bronewsky, in order to carry out his instructions, asked Herr von Jagow for an interview, the latter began by putting him off till late in the afternoon of the 25th, the very moment when the time limit of the ultimatum expired. After pressure, M. Bronewsky was ultimately received a little earlier, only, however, to be told that his proposal would be transmitted without comment to Vienna. Not only did Herr von Jagow refuse to support it, but he added that this step had not been taken soon enough, and that, besides, he thought it inexpedient for Austria to yield at the last moment: he even feared that such a move might "increase Servia's assurance". In Vienna, when the Russian chargé d'affaires called at the Foreign Office, Count Berchtold happened to be away; he was received by the general secretary "whose manner however was freezing" and who, whilst assuring him that his communication should be transmitted, warned him without hesitation that the refusal would be categorical.[37]

---

[33] *Y. B.*, nos 36 and 37.

[34] There is no trace of this first attempt at conciliation either in the *White Book* or in the Preface.

[35] *O. B.*, no 4.

[36] *O. B.*, nos 15 and 16; *B. Cor.*, no 29.

[37] *O. B.*, nos 14 and 11; *Y. B.*, no 45. — Neither is there any trace in the *White Book* of this second attempt at conciliation and of its rebuff.

From this moment, all that could be done was to await the Servian reply to Austria.

The Servian Reply. The reply was anxiously awaited, for it was generally believed that Servia would not surrender, the Austrian demands being thought so exorbitant. All that could be hoped was, that she would not reply by an absolute refusal and thus put an end to all negotiations.

On the 25th of July at 5.45 p. m. she sent her reply which was a complete surrender.

Servia undertook to make the solemn declaration demanded of her and in the exact terms prescribed. As for the ten remaining articles of the ultimatum two, but only two, were not accepted except with certain reservations. These concerned the co-operation of foreign officials.

The Servian Government indicated that it did not grasp clearly in what that co-operation could consist with regard to "the destruction of the subversive movement". However it declared itself ready to admit such co-operation "as agrees with the principles of international law, with criminal procedure and with good neighbourly relations" (art. 5).

The participation of Austro-Hungarian authorities in the judicial enquiry was also judged impossible; as it would be "a violation of the Constitution and of the law of criminal procedure". Nevertheless, added the note "in concrete cases, communications as to the results of the investigation in question might be given to the Austro-Hungarian representatives" (art. 6).

Servia pledged herself to conform to all the other demands made by Austria. With regard to the measures to be taken against the intrigues of the press, the Servian Government did point out that the present state of the law left it provisionally unarmed, to provoke hatred of Austria not being legally a crime, and the confiscation of publications where these intrigues might be produced not being allowed by the Constitution. But it undertook at the first convocation of the Skouptchina and at the approaching revision of the Constitution to have the necessary laws voted.

Finally, in case the Austrian Government should not be satisfied with its reply, the Servian Government declared itself "*ready, as always, to accept a pacific understanding, either by referring this question to the decision of the International Tribunal of the Hague, or to the great Powers*".

Thus, even as regards the points reserved, the door stood wide open for an understanding. It can scarcely be doubted that this unhoped-for submission was due to the action of Russia. In fact, on the 27th of July, that is to say at a date when peace was still more compromised than at the moment at which we have arrived, the Czar of Russia, in reply to an appeal made to him on the 24th by the Crown Prince of Servia, sent him urgent counsels of prudence and moderation. "My Government," said the Czar, "is working hard to smoothe present difficulties. I do not doubt that your Highness and the Royal Government will facilitate this task *by neglecting nothing to arrive at a solution which will prevent the horrors of a new war*, whilst at the same time safeguarding the dignity of Servia. As long as there is the least hope of avoiding bloodshed, all our efforts must be directed to that end".

II. — The diplomatic rupture and the declaration of war against Servia (July 25th–28th).

Peace might have been thought assured. Herr von Jagow himself recognised on the 29th of July, that "he saw (in the Servian reply) a possible basis for negotiations". Unfortunately Austria was not content with the success she had obtained. The note was sent at 5.45 p. m. A few moments afterwards the Austrian minister broke off diplomatic relations. He had not even taken the time materially necessary to look into a matter which might have such serious consequences. He must therefore have received orders to break off in any case. This rupture was, besides, so entirely in conformity with the wishes of the Government and with public opinion that the news was greeted with enthusiasm in Vienna and in Berlin.[38]

Even at this moment Austria did not feel any need to justify her determination; it was only on the 28th of July that a note of explanation, and a very short one, was given to M. Bienvenu-Martin. The Servian reply was declared to be entirely unsatisfactory on three essential points.[39]

The reason given by Servia for not admitting in principle the participation of Austro-Hungarian representatives in the prosecution of the accessories to the plot residing on Servian territory, was considered a vain excuse. It was said that Austria had demanded this co-operation for "police investigations" and not for "judicial enquiries" and that Servia, by substituting one expression for another, was equivocating.

Secondly, it was declared that the measures proposed for putting an end to the intriguing of the press were equivalent to a refusal, for actions against the press are rarely successful, and

---

[38] *Y. B.*, no 47; *B. Cor.*, no 41.

[39] *Y. B.*, nos 75 *bis*.

besides, no definite date was fixed for the amendments that it was promised should be introduced into the law.

Finally, in the article relative to anti-Austrian societies, though Servia promised to dissolve the Narodna Odbrana Society, she deliberately omitted to consider the possibility of that society being formed again under another name.[40]

But it is difficult not to see what an enormous difference there is between the insignificance of these grievances and the gravity of the decision taken by Austria.

As regards the last point more especially the Austrian complaints were inexplicable, for Servia had pledged herself to dissolve not only the Narodna Odbrana but "any other society directing its efforts against Austria". The name had therefore nothing to do with the matter.

Regarding the measures to be taken against the press, Austria, to prove the Servian proposal a disguised refusal, ought at least to have indicated some other legal procedure which would be more efficacious. Yet she indicated none. In fact we cannot see how it was possible to punish an act hitherto unpunishable without making a new law declaring it an offence, nor how publications could be legally confiscated if the Constitution forbade such confiscation. Or was Austria really asking Servia to act illegally and arbitrarily?

The only serious point in dispute was, therefore, that which concerned the collaboration of the Austro-Hungarian authorities. But if the difficulty raised by Servia came merely from the fact, that the word "enquiry" had been wrongly substituted for "investigation", was it not possible to ascertain first by pacific means whether there had not been a misunderstanding on her part instead of at once taking up arms to decide the question?

---

[40] This explanation and those which follow are borrowed, not from the note received by M Bienvenu-Martin which states the Austrian grievances without justifying them, but from the *White Book* (p. 23 and following pages). The Servian reply is accompanied in it by a commentary of Austrian origin, the aim of which is to prove that the concessions of Servia are purely apparent.

A singular step on the part of Germany. – At this phase of the crisis, the general attitude of Austria and Germany remained what it had previously been. We shall soon have the proof of this. Meanwhile, Germany took at this moment a singular step which deserves our attention.

On the 26th of July, the morrow of the rupture, Herr von Schoen called on M. Bienvenu-Martin and renewed the request that Germany had already made to Sir E. Grey. "Austria", said he, "has informed Russia that she is not seeking territorial aggrandizement; she merely wishes to ensure her tranquillity". Peace would therefore be certain if Russia would refrain from all intervention, that is to say if she would allow Austria to inflict on Servia the treatment the latter deserves. Let France then use her influence to this end in St. Petersburg and she will be listened to". "Germany", he added, "is on the side of France in her ardent desire for the maintenance of peace". This affirmation of solidarity was again insisted upon at the end of the conversation.[41]

The same day at seven o'clock in the evening, the Ambassador returned to the Ministry. He went to the political Department and asked that a communiqué on the afternoon's conversation might be sent to the press in order to avoid any erroneous comments. He even proposed to draw up this note in the following terms: "The German Ambassador and the Minister for Foreign Affairs had a further interview in the course of the afternoon, during which they examined *in the most friendly spirit and with a feeling of pacific solidarity*, the means which might be employed for the maintenance of general peace".[42] The morning of the 27th he addressed a letter on the same subject to the Political Director in which, after having again summarised the conversation of the day before, he added: "Note well the phrase as to the solidarity of pacific sentiments. It is not a meaningless phrase".[43]

---

[41] *Y. B.*, no 56.

[42] *Y. B.*, no 57.

[43] *Y. B.*, no 62.

Naturally, the French Government refused to comply with a request which could only deceive public opinion; for even supposing that Germany did share the pacific sentiments of France, the two Governments did not mean peace in the same way. Germany wished that Russia exclusively should be influenced, so that the Vienna Cabinet might have a free hand; France could only lend herself to action which would be undertaken at the same time in Vienna and St. Petersburg. But then, why ask for a public declaration that agreed so little with the real state of affairs? Was this not an attempt to make people believe that France was acting in concert with Germany, and thus to compromise the French Government with Russia and disorganise the dual alliance? In this way, Russia was being isolated while by means of pacific assurances, which were merely verbal, a kind of pretext was being prepared for throwing upon the allies the responsibility of the war, should it break out, as was now to be feared.

Two further attempts at conciliation repulsed by Germany and Austria. – Whilst by this ambiguous attempt, Germany was pursuing only her private interests, the Powers of the Triple Entente, supported by Italy, were working hard in the interests of peace. Diplomatic relations were broken off but war was not declared; it was, perhaps, still possible to stop the conflict before the opening of hostilities.

From the very beginning, Sir E. Grey had laid down with perfect clearness England's position in the discussion.

In itself the Austro-Servian war did not concern him, and if Austria were able to settle her difference with Servia, without the intervention of Russia, he need not interfere.[44] But he could not lose sight of the fact that if war between the two countries should be declared, it would be impossible for Russia to look on indifferent to the crushing of Servia. Now, this intervention of Russia, by drawing in that of Germany, threatened the European peace which England had every interest in safeguarding.

---

44 *B. Cor.*, no 10.

Though Servia concerned her little, peace concerned her greatly. There was, it is true, a means of attaining this end which it seemed could have been very efficacious; that would have been to consolidate in advance with Russia and France and to announce that in case of war, England would support the two allies. In fact, it was possible to believe that if Germany knew that the English fleet would be against her, she might be less arbitrary. M. Sazonoff did not fail to point this out to the English Government.[45]

However Sir Ed. Grey refused several times to engage himself on this point in any way which would bind him for the future. As long as Austria and Servia alone were concerned, public opinion in England would not have understood going to war on a question which did not directly affect English interests.[46] Without doubt if the conflict became general it was more than likely that England would be drawn into it; but her attitude would depend on circumstances, and for that reason she was anxious to retain her liberty of action. This implied that, if Russia precipitated matters, England would not be responsible for the consequences that might result.[47] Sir Ed. Grey added that he would have more authority in negotiating with the German Government, if he did not announce himself in advance as an eventual adversary.[48]

He was moreover particularly qualified to undertake these negotiations, for the absence of precise obligations between the Governments in question, permitted him to view the situation with perfect impartiality. He recognised that Austria might have serious grievances against Servia;[49] he even went so far as to say that the latter needed to be taught a lesson. But he considered that, under the pretext of humiliating Servia, the

---

45 *B. Cor.*, no 6.

46 *B. Cor.*, no 24.

47 *B. Cor.*, no 17.

48 *B. Cor.*, no 44.

49 *B. Cor.*, no 5.

humiliation of Russia must not be involved.[50] The Servian reply seemed to him to give satisfaction to Austria further than could have been expected. He saw in it at least a basis for discussion and reflection.[51]

On all these points an understanding was easy with Russia. She, too, recognised that Austria had grounds for complaint and that "some of her demands were reasonable enough", but that others were impraticable, at least at the moment; these were the demands which demanded alterations in the laws regarding the press and the societies. There were some also which were incompatible with Servia's dignity as an independent State.[52] "If", said M. Sazonoff to the Austrian Ambassador, "you have pursued no other aim than the protection of your territory against the agitation of Servian Anarchists", your intentions are legitimate, "but the step to which you have had recourse is not defensible. *Take back your ultimatum*", he concluded, "*modify its form, and I will guarantee the result*".[53] In precise terms, all that he asked was "that the territorial integrity of Servia should be guaranteed, and that her rights as a sovereign State should be respected so that she should not become Austria's vassal". Within these conditions he declared himself ready "to use all his influence at Belgrade to induce the Servian Government to go as far as possible in giving satisfaction to Austria".[54]

Two means were tried in order to arrive at this result.

Taking up, but in more detail, the idea he had expressed from the very beginning, Sir Ed. Grey proposed that the four great Powers not directly concerned in the debate, should intervene as mediators. The Ambassadors of France, Germany and Italy should be authorised to meet in conference with Sir Ed. Grey for the purpose of discovering a way out; but Servia,

---

50 *B. Cor.*, no 90.

51 *B. Cor.*, no 46.

52 *O. B.*, no 25.

53 *Y. B.*, no 54.

54 *B. Cor.*, no 55.

Russia and Austria should be induced to "abstain from all active military operations" pending the results of the conference.[55] This procedure seemed to offer many advantages: Servia would submit more easily to Europe than to Austria and, by gaining time, the chances of a pacific solution would be increased.

The idea was accepted eagerly by France and Italy.[56] M. Sazonoff declared himself equally ready to give his adherence. But in the meantime he had attempted to come to an understanding by other means; he had offered to Austria to confer directly with her, without having recourse to any intermediary. He was therefore obliged to await the answer to his proposal. But even should the conversation he desired take place, he thought it advisable that he should keep in contact with the Powers and that these should keep in touch with each other. Consequently these two plans, far from excluding, complemented each other.[57]

England soon knew the fate of her plan: Germany absolutely refused to have anything to do with it. She indeed accepted, in vague terms, the general principle of a mediation on the part of the four Powers, but refused a conference. It would, she said, be making Austria and Russia appear before a court of arbitration, which seemed to her inadmissible. In vain, Sir E. Grey and the English Ambassador in Berlin replied that it would not be an arbitration, but a private and informal discussion to ascertain what suggestion could be made for a settlement.[58] Herr von Jagow maintained his position without in any way justifying it. On the 27th of July he had a conversation with M. J. Cambon on this very subject, which, at one moment, took a pathetic turn. As he repeated once more that it was impossible to "call together a conference to discuss the affairs of Austria and Russia", M. Cambon expostulated. Sir E. Grey's pro-

---

55 *B. Cor.*, no 36.

56 *B. Cor.*, nos 49 and 51.

57 *B. Cor.*, nos 53 and 55.

58 *B. Cor.*, nos 43 and 67.

posal, said he, was above a question of form. What was important was the association of England and France with Germany and Italy in working for peace; this association, once formed, could "show itself in common action in Vienna and in St. Petersburg", and it would be a fine and salutary example for four Powers belonging to the two groups, instead of perpetually opposing each other, to act together to prevent the conflict. It would thus be seen that a European spirit really existed. Herr von Jagow gave evasive answers; he urged his engagements with Austria; he pretended that he had not yet read the Servian reply, though it was known throughout Europe (it was now the 27th of July). At last, tired and no doubt irritated by these obscure and elusive replies, M. Cambon suddenly asked his interlocutor *"if Germany wanted war"*. And as the latter assured him of his good intentions, the French Ambassador added: "you must then act up to them. When you read the Servian reply, I beg you in the name of humanity, to weigh the terms with your conscience, and do not personally assume a portion of the responsibility for the catastrophe you are allowing to be prepared".[59] To this appeal there was no response.

The Russian proposal fared no better. The German Government had declared several times that it favoured this proposal; after all it had no reason for opposing it, since Germany was in no way involved.[60] But when asked to support it at Vienna and to invite in a friendly way the Austrian Government to "accept this means of reconciliation", Herr von Jagow replied "that he could not advise Austria to yield".[61] Austria, too, did nothing towards entering into Russia's views of the question. Already M. Sazonoff and the Austrian Ambassador had had a private conversation and the result had seemed satisfactory: they virtually agreed as to the nature of the guarantees which could be legitimately demanded of Servia.[62] Under these

---

59 *Y. B.*, no 74.

60 *Y. B.*, no 74; *O. B.*, no 49.

61 *O. B.*, no 38.

62 *O. B.*, no 32; *B. Cor.*, no 56.

conditions, M. Sazonoff asked Count Berchtold to furnish the Austrian Ambassador with full powers and instructions so that the discussion begun privately, might be continued officially. But on the 28th M. Sazonoff had not yet received an answer and he began to realise that "Austria did not wish to talk".[63] In fact, at the same moment, Count Berchtold informed the Russian Ambassador at Vienna that he would have to decline to enter into a discussion on the terms of the Austrian note.[64] This was equivalent to declining the very principle of the negotiations.[65]

Besides, that very day the event took place which it was so desirable to avoid or delay. After the rupture of the diplomatic relations, Austria confined herself to mobilising; she even let it be understood that hostilities would not begin at once. Now, on the 28th, as if it were desired to cut short the negotiations in progress, war was declared and military operations began at once.[66] This decision was all the more regrettable as the Servian delegate at Rome was, with the Italian Minister for Foreign Affairs, taking steps of a nature to facilitate peace. "If", said he, "explanations were given regarding the mode in which Austrian agents will require to intervene under Art. 5 and Art. 6, *Servia might still accept the whole Austrian note*".[67] The Marquis of San Giuliano, on his side, pointed out that if Austria, for reasons of dignity, refused to give these details to Servia, she could without any difficulty make them known to the Powers, who would transmit them to the Servian Government. The question as to whether the words "enquiry" and "investigation" were or were not synonymous might thus be elucidated otherwise than by arms.

---

[63] *Y. B.*, no 82.

[64] *B. Cor.*, no 61.

[65] *O. B.*, no 50.

[66] Already before the declaration of war, the Austrians had fired on two Servian steamers and had damaged them; two Servian merchant-vessels had been captured by a Hungarian monitor (*B. Cor.*, no 65).

[67] *B. Cor.*, no 64.

Why, then, had this violent resolution been taken in the midst of negotiations which it seemed destined to cut short? Among the suspicions it arouses, wrote M. Paléologue on the 28th, "the most disturbing is that Germany may have urged her (Austria) to aggression against Servia, so as to be able herself to enter the lists against France and Russia in circumstances which, she supposes, ought to be the most favourable for her and in conditions which have been considered in advance".[68] We merely reproduce this opinion as information for our readers.

---

[68] *Y. B.*, no 83.

III. — The first ultimatum of Germany to Russia (July the 29th and 30th).

Thus the more the crisis developed the more remote seamed a pacific solution. In vain England, Russia, France and Italy joined their forces to prevent the dreaded result; each of the phases we have been describing was a step towards war. This was indeed so imminent that it all but broke out on the 30th of July.

The Triple Entente and Italy continue the negotiations. The evasive attitudes of Germany. – Everyone thought that if Servia were attacked, Russia would be obliged to march at once to her assistance.[69] And yet, even after the declaration of war, the conciliatory intentions of M. Sazonoff remained unchanged. On the 29th of July M. Paléologue informed the French Government "that the Russian Government acquiesces in any step which may be proposed to it by France and England for the safeguarding of peace".[70] The same language was used in London.[71] All that M. Sazonoff asked was that no time should be lost so as to prevent Austria from taking advantage of this delay to crush Servia.

Judging by appearances it was possible to think the chances of peace still good, for Germany's language at this moment seemed to take a more favourable turn.

It seemed as though a sudden change had taken place and as if the Berlin Cabinet had now decided to exercise its influence at Vienna in favour of peace. In fact on the morning of the 29th, Herr von Schoen, informally it is true, went to inform M. Bienvenu-Martin that the German Government was using its influence to persuade the Austrian Government to make known

---

69 *B. Cor.*, no 11.

70 *Y. B.*, no 86.

71 *B Cor.*, no 78; *O. B.*, no 59.

the aim and extent of the operations in Servia. "The Berlin Cabinet", he added, "hopes to receive details which will be such as to give satisfaction to Russia... When it is known how far Austria wishes to go, there will be a basis for discussion".[72] The same communication was made at St. Petersburg[73] and at London.[74] On the 30th the German Chancellor said to Sir E. Goschen that he "was pressing the button" to put into action the mechanism of mediation; he was even not sure whether he had made the mistake of going too far in urging moderation at Vienna, that matters had been precipitated rather than otherwise.[75]

These fair words, though somewhat vague, might seem reassuring. Unfortunately neither in the diplomatic documents nor in the march of events could there be seen any trace of the conciliatory influence that Germany pretended to be exercising almost to excess.

The German Government has published a *White Book* exclusively intended to prove that it is not responsible for the war, and that it did all that was humanly possible in favour of peace. The best way to prove this statement would have been to publish the despatches in which it gave its Ambassador at Vienna, Herr von Tschirsky, these pacific instructions. Now, out of the 27 documents contained in the *White Book*, *there is not a single one which has this object in view*. Nowhere is there any question of any influence being exercised on the Austrian Government to urge it to be more moderate in its demands. We certainly see the German Chancellor, in a telegram of the 27th of July, transmit to Vienna M. Sazonoff's and Sir E. Grey's proposals of which we have already spoken, but he did not support them in any way; then one finds a telegram dated the 28th in which Herr von Tschirsky replies that Count Berchtold refuses them as too late in arriving, war against

---

[72] *Y. B.*, no 94.

[73] *B. Cor.*, no 93, 2 and annexe.

[74] *B. Cor.*, no 81.

[75] *B. Cor.*, no 107.

Servia having been already declared. And that is all. No doubt, a diplomatic collection generally contains only selected documents. But it would seem surprising that the German Chancellery should have omitted precisely those which it had the greatest advantage in publishing.

Are Germany's pacific inclinations, in default of written instructions, shown by acts?

Since Austria had absolutely refused direct negotiations with Russia, there was now only one means left: that was to fall back on the English plan and for the four disinterested Powers to intervene by a conference, or by any other method. Circumstances seemed favourable. Now that Austria had obtained some satisfaction by bombarding Belgrade she might perhaps be less hostile to the idea of allowing Europe to settle the question. Moreover the new concessions that Servia said she was willing to make (see above p. 26) might render an arrangement easier.[76] So M. Sazonoff asked at once that the English proposal might be taken up.[77]

Sir E. Grey spoke of it again to Prince Lichnowsky, who, however, gave the same refusal as before, and the same reasons as a justification. It seemed to him inadmissible that Austria should be brought before a European Court. But Sir Ed. Grey insisted. Germany had accepted the principle of mediation. If then the words "conference" and "arbitration" frightened her, it was for her to say under what form she considered that mediation possible which she herself considered necessary. Any formula suggested by her would be gratefully agreed to, should it allow of the maintenance of peace.[78] Germany was thus obliged to renounce the vague generalities in which she had persisted until then and to make at last some definite proposal. We shall soon see whether the mediation of which she spoke was but a word, or whether, on the contrary, she saw in it a

---

[76] *B. Cor.*, no 90.

[77] *O. B.*, no 48.

[78] *Y. B.*, no 98; *B. Cor.*, no 84.

concrete reality. As M. Cambon said, "she was driven into a corner".[79]

Without doubt she found the question embarrassing for, on the 30th, she had not yet answered it; and yet the moment had arrived when hours and even minutes were of inestimable value.[80] When M. Cambon questioned Herr von Jagow as to this delay, the latter made excuses, replying that "in order to gain time" he had decided to act directly and that he "had asked Austria on what basis conversations with her could take place".[81] He even boasted that he had advised her to declare openly that her exclusive object in opening hostilities was to secure the guarantees necessary to her existence.[82] But even had Austria consented to make this declaration, the progress of the negotiations would not have been facilitated, for the Austro-Hungarian Government had already stated many times that it only asked for indispensable guarantees. Unfortunately it was still unknown what was meant by these. In a word, by adopting this manner of proceeding, Germany evaded, instead of answering, the embarrassing question she was asked; she avoided saying how she understood this action of the Powers which she admitted in principle but which she, in reality, in all its practical forms, set on one side.

Yet Germany had a very simple means of working for peace, which was to bring her weight to bear on the Vienna Cabinet and to persuade it to lay claim only to acceptable guarantees. Russia contented herself with asking Austria to respect Servia's rights as a sovereign State in addition to her territorial integrity. The important point was, in fact, that Servia should not become politically dependent on Austria. Let Austria give assurances regarding this point and peace was almost certain. But when M. Sazonoff asked the German Government to help him to obtain them, he met with a refusal.

---

79 *Y. B.*, no 81.

80 *Y. B.*, no 108.

81 *Y. B.*, no 109.

82 *B. Cor.*, no 75.

Herr von Pourtalès, with whom he had a conversation on this subject, merely replied that he would transmit his request to Berlin, but that he could do no more. He even added that to make such a proposal to Germany was to ask her "to do with regard to Austria what Austria was reproached with wishing to do with regard to Servia; it was to interfere in her sovereign rights. By declaring that she had no territorial pretensions, Austria had pledged herself to take into account Russian interests, a great concession on the part of a State engaged in war. She ought therefore to be allowed to settle her affairs with Servia alone. It would be time enough when the peace conference was held to come back to the question as to whether the sovereignty of Servia should be spared and in what measure".[83]

The real policy of Germany, then, agreed in no way with her language; whilst protesting an ardent desire to safeguard peace, she rejected every means proposed for reaching that end and suggested none herself. The principles which guided the German Government explain this ambiguity. According to it, in effect, Russia had no grounds for intervening, but ought to stand aloof from Servia; since Austria had promised to respect Servian territory nothing more was required of her. Now, this is what Russia could not admit. The peace which Germany said she was so desirous to bring about, was thus dependent on a condition which rendered war inevitable. The mediation she was offering, was the reverse of mediation; for the part of a

---

[83] *W. B.*, p. 9. — We read, however, in the Preface to the *While Book:* "At our suggestion the Austro-Hungarian Ambassador received instructions on the 29th July to enter into conversation with M. Sazonoff. Count Szapary was authorised to explain to the Russian Minister the note addressed to Servia, and to accept any suggestion from Russia, as well as to discuss with M. Sazonoff all questions concerning Austro-Russian relations" (p. 10). *We have just seen what language the German Ambassador used to M. Sazonoff on the 29th July: there is no trace of the conciliatory disposition which, at the same moment, the Government at Berlin is said to have suggested to the Cabinet at Vienna.* Besides, on the 29th Count Berchtold had just refused any direct conversation with Russia. We see what respect the *White Book* has for the truth. Besides, it, of course, does not quote any document in support of its attention.

mediator does not consist in disregarding the interests and claims of one of the suitors in the case. She spoke of calming the conflict, but forgot the difficulty which was the origin of it. She uttered the word conciliation but understood by it the entire submission of one of the two adversaries. Nowhere is there more glaring evidence of this contradiction than in two telegrams sent by the German Emperor at about this time, to the Czar of Russia. Having returned from a cruise on the 26th, William II telegraphed on the 28th to his cousin to tell him that he was going to use his influence at Vienna; but at the same time he declared emphatically that Austria's demands were entirely justified; and as the Czar, in his reply, had protested against this assertion, William II telegraphed again to maintain it. He added imperiously that, in the Austro-Servian war, Russia ought to play the part of a spectator, and that, moreover, it was easy for her to do so.[84]

Finally, a proof of what Germany's disposition really was, is that, during the very days that these negotiations were taking place, she was preparing to take action, which, if accomplished, would immediately have caused war.

The first ultimatum of Germany to Russia. — From the very beginning of the crisis, the Russian Government had been obliged to give its attention to the military measures which might become necessary. On the 25th July at a Cabinet Council presided over by the Czar, the mobilisation of thirteen army corps was considered, destined to act eventually against Austria. However it was not to become effective unless Austria should take up arms against Servia, and only after notification by the Minister of Foreign Affairs.[85] On the 29th July, it was judged that the moment had arrived. War against Servia had begun the day before; moreover Austria refused all compromises and all conversations; in fact she had already mobilised eight army corps and had even begun to mass troops in Galicia

[84] *W. B.*, nos 20 and 22.

[85] *Y. B.*, no 50.

on the Russian frontier.[86] It was therefore decided to mobilise four military districts.

This decision was officially communicated to the German Government in the most friendly terms; it was assured that Russia had no aggressive intention against Germany.[87] Austria was also informed that the mobilisation implied no hostile intention, but only "aimed at marking the intention and the rights of the Czar to express his view in the settlement of the Servian question". The Austrian Government, too, did not resent it; Count Berchtold and M. Schebeko, the Russian Ambassador at Vienna, even had a conversation on the 30th during which very pacific proposals were exchanged.[88] We shall speak of these again later.

But Germany, although she was not menaced, took matters very differently. Even during the day of the 29th, Count de Pourtalès went to tell M. Sazonoff that, if Russia did not stop her military preparations, the German army would receive orders to mobilise; and events will show us that, for Germany mobilisation meant war.[89] Moreover the tone in which this notification was given, said M. Sazonoff, "decided the Russian Government to order that very evening (July 29th-30th) the mobilisation of the thirteen army corps destined to operate against Austria".[90] Thus the German Government did not shrink from letting war loose upon Europe on account of a measure which did not concern it, which was only directed against Austria, and nevertheless which Austria accepted without protest.

---

86 *Y. B.*, nos 95, 97, 101.

87 *B.* Cor., no 70.

88 *Y. B.*, no 104.

89 *Cf. W. B.*, Pref., p. 7.

90 *Y. B.*, no 100. — However, M. Viviani having expressed to him the desire, that no military measure should be taken that might give Germany a pretext for general mobilisation, M. Sazonoff let him know that in the course of the night the General Staff had suspended some of the military measures that might have caused a misunderstanding (*Y. B.*, no 102).

And the threat was very near to being carried out. During the evening of the 29th, an extraordinary Council was held at Potsdam under the presidency of the Emperor. The military authorities had been summoned to it. Decisions were taken which were not made public, but which, certainly, were not in favour of peace; for the Chancellor sent in haste for the English Ambassador, Sir E. Goschen, and after having expressed to him the fear that a European conflagration might become inevitable, made "a high bid to insure the neutrality of England". If, said he, Great Britain would consent to stand aloof, the Imperial Government was ready to give every assurance that, in case of victory, it would not seek any territorial aggrandisement at the expense of continental France; he refused, however, to make the same engagement regarding the French colonies. At the same time, he promised that Germany would respect the neutrality of Holland, if it were equally respected by the other belligerents. As for Belgium, "it depended upon the actions of France what operations Germany might be forced to enter upon in Belgium"; in any case, if Belgium did not side against Germany, she should be evacuated after the war. Finally, he ended by reminding Sir Ed. Goschen that ever since he had been Chancellor the object of his policy had been to bring about an understanding with England. "He trusted that these assurances might form the basis of that understanding which he so much desired. He had in his mind a general neutrality agreement between Germany and England . . . and an assurance of British neutrality in the conflict would enable him to look forward to realisation of his desire".[91]

The fact that this conversation took place in haste, immediately after the conference at Potsdam, proves that it had been decided on by resolutions taken during the course of that conference and that the question which the Chancellor discussed with the Ambassador was considered by him as being exceptionally urgent. Now this question presupposed a declaration of war. Measures, then, had just been taken at Potsdam which rendered war imminent. And, in fact, on the 30th,

---

[91] *B. Cor.*, no 85.

towards one o'clock in the afternoon, the *Lokal Anzeiger* issued a special edition in which there was to be found the decree giving the orders for general mobilisation.[92]

However an hour afterwards, Herr von Jagow telephoned to the Ambassador to deny the news, and the Government ordered the copies of the newspaper, in which it had been published, to be seized. But the *Lokal Anzeiger*, a semi-official organ, would not have prepared a special edition to announce a measure of such gravity, had it not really been taken. After the deed was done, it had been decided to go back on it, but the Government forgot to inform the newspaper. This sudden change is explained, moreover, by another step taken by M. de Pourtalès; this same night of the 29th-30th, he returned to M. Sazonoff, and, though he urged again that Russia should cease her military preparations, it was in a tone much less categorical and in no way threatening. He merely asked under what conditions Russia would suspend her mobilisation. The ultimatum was withdrawn.[93]

The conversation that Herr von Bethmann-Hollweg had had some hours before with Sir E. Goschen, had, most probably, much to do with this change of attitude. The English Ambassador had, in fact, replied with the greatest reserve to the warm appeal that had been addressed to him, and to the offers that had been made. He confined himself to declaring that, in his opinion, Sir E. Grey would not care to bind himself to any course of action but would desire to retain full liberty.[94] A little later in the night, the Chancellor was informed, by a telegram from London, of a conversation that had taken place, that very day, between Sir E. Grey and the German Ambassador. Sir E. Grey had taken the initiative of warning Prince Lichnowsky that, if war broke out, and if France were drawn into it in the wake of Germany and Russia, he would not bind himself "to stand aside". He had added, moreover, that he did

---

[92] *O. B.*, no 61.

[93] *Y. B.*, no 103.

[94] *B. Cor.*, no 85.

not wish to use anything in the nature of a threat; for that reason he declined to specify the circumstances in which England might intervene. He simply desired to preserve his liberty of action; but he did not wish the friendly tone of his conversations with the Prince to mislead the German Government into supposing that England would not take action in any case. Above all, he was anxious not to lay himself open in the future "to the reproach that if they had not been so misled the course of things might have been different".[95] This conversation, which confirmed the preceding, was still more significant and Herr von Bethmann-Hollweg easily understood all its import.[96]

Germany was essentially anxious for England to remain neutral;[97] the steps taken by the Chancellor is the best proof of this and we shall find others. The only reason by which she could justify at this moment a general mobilisation against Russian was untenable, since Austria, the only Power interested, made no objections to the Russian preparations. It was therefore to be feared that war declared under these conditions, might be one of those circumstances of which Sir E. Grey had spoken and which would force him to intervene. This was why it was resolved to suspend the measures already decided on and to wait.[98]

A further pacific proposal on the part of Russia rejected by Germany. – But this incident offered M. Sazonoff another opportunity of showing the sincerity of his pacific intentions.

During the course of his second visit to the Minister for Foreign Affairs, Count de Pourtalès had repeated once more that the promise given by Austria not to encroach on Servian

---

95 *B. Cor.*, no 89.

96 *B. Cor.*, no 98, *in fine*.

97 *B. Cor.*, nos 75 and 76.

98 In the German *White Book*, as in the Preface, there is no trace of this ultimatum nor of the events with which it is connected.

territory, ought to satisfy Russia. "It is not only the territorial integrity of Servia which we must safeguard", replied M. Sazonoff, "but also her independence and her sovereignty". Then he added: "The situation is too serious for me not to tell you all that is in my mind. By intervening at St. Petersburg, while refusing to intervene at Vienna, Germany is only seeking to gain time so as to allow Austria to crush the little Servian kingdom before Russia can come to its aid. But the Emperor Nicholas is so anxious to prevent war that in his name I am going to make you a fresh proposal: *If Austria recognising that her dispute with Servia has assumed the character of a question of European interest, declares herself ready to eliminate from her ultimatum the clauses which are damaging to the sovereignty of Servia, Russia will undertake to stop all military preparations*".[99]

Count de Pourtalès promised to transmit this proposal to his Government. But the same day, Herr von Jagow, when informed of it, said, without even consulting Vienna, that he considered such a proposal inacceptable to Austria.[100]

To sum up, there is at this period a marked contrast between the words and the deeds of the German Government. We may indeed ask ourselves if its words were not intended to cover its deeds and to make people believe that the measures taken or prepared at this moment by Germany, were forced upon her by the malignity of her adversaries, in spite of herself and of the pacific sentiments which her words professed.

---

[99] *Y. B.*, no 103; *O. B.*, no 60.

[100] *O. B.*, no 63; *Y. B.*, no 107. – In the German *White Book*, there is no trace of this further attempt at conciliation.

IV. — The declaration of war against Russia and against France (July 31st–Aug. 3rd).

We arrive now at the crisis. In consequence of the insecurity and mutual distrust in which all the peoples of Europe were living, the question of mobilisation arose afresh in a more acute form and the result was war.

The second ultimatum of Germany to Russia. — Austria had as yet only mobilised a part of her troops; but on the 31st July, at an early hour, general mobilisation was decreed; all men from 19 to 42 years of age were called out.[101] The measure was a grave one. No doubt Count Berchtold thought he could take this step without inconvenience; for, only the day before, M. Schebeko and he had agreed that military preparations made on either side need not be considered as acts of hostility.

At this news, Russia judged it natural that she should take similar precautions. Besides she knew that, for some days, Germany was preparing for mobilisation: the German fleet off Norway returned to Germany; the reservists had received orders not to absent themselves (cf. above, p. 11); officers on leave were recalled, owners of motor-cars were invited to hold these at the disposal of the military authorities; important movements of troops were taking place near to the Gulf of Finland, etc. Under these conditions, and especially taking into consideration the extreme slowness of the Russian mobilisation, it seemed impossible to wait any longer. On the 31st July,

---

[101] *Y. B.*, no 115.

towards the middle of the day, a general mobilisation of the army and navy was ordered.[102]

Austria received the news without raising any objection; at this very moment, as we shall soon see, the relations between the two countries were improving and from that hour went on improving. But in Berlin the protests were vigorous and were immediately translated into action. As early as 2 p. m., the German Emperor had sent a telegram to the Czar of a very threatening nature. He did not yet mention the Russian mobilisation, but complained of the military measures that were said to have been taken against him on his Eastern frontier. He announced that he would be obliged to take "the same defensive precautions", and without saying that war would necessarily result, insinuated that it was inevitable if Russia did not cease arming; he declined all responsibility beforehand and threw it entirely on the Emperor Nicholas.[103]

A state of danger of war (Kriegsgefahrzustand) was also decreed; it is even possible that the decree preceded the telegram. The result of this measure was, in effect, to break off the

---

[102] *B. Cor.*, no 113; *Y. B.*, no 118. — This important fact that the general mobilisation of Austria was anterior to the general mobilisation of Russia is nowhere mentioned in the *White Book*. Yet that it was anterior is certain. It is proved not only by the explicit telegram sent by M. Paléologue, but also by the report addressed to his Government by Sir M. de Bunsen after his return to England (*B. Cor.*, no 101). There is indeed a telegram from the same ambassador fixing the general mobilisation of the army and the fleet for Aug. 1st (*B. Cor.*, no 127); but by that is meant that Aug. 1st was the first day of the mobilisation; the decree was promulgated the day before.

The German press makes very much of a letter written by a Belgian diplomatic agent, a M. de l'Escaille, which was intercepted by the German *cab t oir*. {?} In this letter, M. de l'Escaille expressed sentiments somewhat favourable to Germany, saying that she had done all in her power to prevent war. Using fact shows what faith we may have in the source from which Mr de l'Escaille draws his information; he says in his letter, dated July 30th, that the decree for general mobilisation was *published* on the 30th at 4 a. m., which is certainly inaccurate. And yet the date of a publication of this kind can easily be verified.

[103] *W. B.*, Pref., p. 13.

relations between Germany and other countries, and allowed the Government to proceed immediately to a real mobilisation. Finally at midnight, the Russian mobilisation having become known at Berlin in the meantime, Count de Pourtalès ordered M. Sazonoff to stop within twelve hours all military preparations "*against Germany as well as against Austria*", otherwise Germany would mobilise.[104] This was an ultimatum of a most offensive form for a great country for it contained a formal summons to Russia to reply within a time limit. Moreover it demanded that she should cease mobilising, not only against Germany, i. e. on the frontier of Eastern Prussia, but even in the South, against Austria who was mobilising all her forces. Even it did not occur to the German Government, that, in any case, bare justice required that the same demand should be addressed to the Government at Vienna; in other words, it was demanded that Russia should put herself vis-à-vis Austria, in such a position of manifest inferiority as Austria herself did not claim. When Sir E. Goschen expressed his surprise to Herr von Jagow that the German Government had thus made the ultimatum more difficult for Russia to accept, Herr von Jagow replied that "it was in order to prevent Russia from saying that all her mobilisation was only directed against Austria".[105]

As Count de Pourtalès said, if it was not war already, it was very near it.

A new formula of compromise accepted by Austria and rejected by Germany. – And yet at this very time, negotiations were going on outside Germany and were taking a more favourable turn than they had yet taken. Were it not for the German threats, one might have thought peace quite near.

We have seen (see above, p. 35) that, on the 30th July, after the partial mobilisation of the Russian army, a conversation of a very conciliatory nature had taken place at Vienna between Count Berchtold and M. Schebeko, but we have not yet men-

---

104 *W. B.*, no 25.

105 *B. Cor.*, no 121.

tioned the most important proposals which were discussed during this interview. Not only had a mutual desire for peace been expressed, but the very root of the difference had been attacked. For the first time the Austro-Servian conflict and the means of settling it were discussed. It was agreed that the conversations begun privately between M. Sazonoff and M. Szapary should be taken up officially; these had been interrupted on the 28th by Count Berchtold, who refused to give his Ambassador the authority necessary to continue them (see above, p. 26): According to the Austrian Minister, this refusal was due to a misunderstanding, but M. Szapary was to be immediately authorised to discuss what settlements would be compatible with the dignity and prestige for which both Empires had an equal concern". Never had Austria made a concession of such importance. On his side, too, the Russian Ambassador stated "that his Government would pay much more regard to the demands of the Austro-Hungarian Monarchy than was supposed".[106]

At this time Germany complained to some of the Powers that the efforts she was making, as she said, to urge peace and moderation at Vienna, were seriously handicapped by the Russian mobilisation against Austria.[107] As a matter of fact, Austria had never shown herself so conciliatory and so much disposed to negotiate. It is impossible to conceive what grounds the German Government can have had for stating what is manifestly contradicted by the facts as they are known to-day. The truth is that the Russian mobilisation marks the critical moment from which we notice a contrast between the attitudes of Germany and Austria which grows stronger and stronger as time goes on. The more the former inclined towards war, the more the latter inclined towards peace.

A new formula elaborated by England and Russia was, moreover, going to make it easier for Austria to change her mind. On the 29th Sir E. Grey, in a conversation with the Ger-

---

106 *Y. B.*, no 104.

107 *B. Cor.*, nos 98, 103, 108; *W. B.*, the Kaiser's telegram, Pref., p. 13.

man Ambassador, suggested that there might still be a way of making mediation more easily acceptable: Austria, as soon as she had occupied part of Servian territory would state "that she would not advance further, pending an effort of the Powers to mediate between her and Russia".[108]

The following day, July 30th, the formula that M. Sazonoff had, the day before, submitted to Germany through Count de Pourtalés and which the German Government had rejected, was communicated to Sir E. Grey (see above, p. 39). It seemed to him that there was some similarity between this proposal and his own, and that with a little good will, M. Sazonoff's formula might be modified so as to correspond with the one he himself had thought of.[109] M. Sazonoff agreed to made this change and proposed the following wording: "If Austria will consent to check the advance of her troops on Servian territory, and if, recognising that the Austro-Servian conflict has become a question of European interest, she will allow the great Powers to look into the matter and decide what satisfaction Servia could afford to the Government of Austria-Hungary without impairing her rights as a sovereign state and her independence – Russia will undertake to maintain her waiting attitude".[110] By proposing this formula M. Sazonoff made a new and difficult sacrifice in the cause of peace, for, as, he recognised in it the fact of the invasion of Servia by Austrian troops, he seemed to admit the right of that invasion.

England and France accepted without hesitation this new proposal. Should Austria in her turn give it her adherence, the ultimatum which had just been addressed to Russia would be

---

[108] *B. Cor.,* no 88. The German Government assured Sir E. Grey that it had transmitted this proposal to Vienna and had given its support to it (*B. Cor.,* nos 88 and 103). We shall see however that when M. Sazonoff had accepted a scarcely modified form of it, Germany would have nothing to do with it. In any case, in the *White Book* there is not a single document which mentions the influence said to have been exercised on Vienna on that occasion.

[109] *B. Cor.*, no 103.

[110] *O. B.*, no 67.

deprived of its object. Germany would obtain satisfaction, for the Russian mobilisation would naturally be stopped as soon as Austria had consented to grant the concessions asked of her. Austria consented at once and informed Germany of the fact.[111] She accepted the principle of mediation; she even agreed to discuss "the substance of the Austrian ultimatum" sent to Servia on the 23rd.[112] In the meantime she multiplied her pacific demonstrations. At Vienna Count Berchtold sent for the Russian Ambassador and "begged him to do his best to remove the wholly erroneous impression in St. Petersburg"; it was wrong, said he, to accuse Austria-Hungary "of having banged the door on all further conversations". He had informed Paris and London that "neither *an infraction of Servian sovereign rights* nor the acquisition of Servian territory was being contemplated by Austria-Hungary".[113] Russia had never asked for more. Thus when Herr von Schoen was made acquainted with these conversations and with their result, of which his Government had left him in ignorance, he could not help recognising that on the 1st Aug. in the morning there was in this "a glimmer of hope".[114]

Probably, if he spoke, in spite of everything, with so much reserve, it was because the silence on the part of his Government regarding these important negotiations did not seem to him a very good omen. In fact, this formula, which all the other States found equitable, which even those the most directly concerned in the conflict had eagerly accepted, was set aside by Germany. In vain on the 1st Aug. the English Ambassador in Berlin did his best to show Herr von Jagow how what strange the situation was: the chief dispute was between Austria and Russia; Germany was only drawn in as Austria's ally; if, therefore, the two States interested were ready to discuss matters, as was evident, it would be illogical for Germany to stand in the

---

111 *B. Cor.*, no 135.

112 *B. Cor.*, no 133.

113 *B. Cor.*, no 137; *O. B.*, no 73.

114 *Y. B.*, no 125.

way of a peaceful solution, "*unless she desired war on her own account*".[115] Herr von Jagow would listen to nothing. Without doubt, said he, "had not Russia mobilised against Germany, all would have been well". Now it was too late. The German Government only saw one thing. A demand had been addressed to Russia; Russia must submit. As for the great concessions made by Austria, Germany did not take them into account, for, according to Herr von Jagow, they were due to German influence. How much it is to be regretted that the despatches have never been published which are said to contain Germany's wise counsels to Vienna. But above all how surprising it is that Germany should have advised such an exemplary moderation during the days from the 29th July to 31st July at the very time that she herself was taking up a distinctly warlike attitude! Besides, whatever may have been the cause of Austria's wise decision, did not anxiety for the general interests of Europe and of civilisation demand that note should be taken of it at once, and that it should be used to the advantage of peace; especially, since at the same time the German Government was obtaining all that it asked for, the demobilisation of Russia?[116]

But at the very moment when this conversation took place, the German mobilisation was already decreed (Aug. 1st).

The declaration of war against Russia. – There is now no further question of Servia and of the Serajevo crime, nor of Austria and her ultimatum. Germany and Russia stand alone face to face.

The ultimatum expired at noon on the 1st Aug. Russia naturally judged it contrary to her dignity to reply within the time limit prescribed to such an arrogant injunction. Yet the Emperor Nicholas did not want war to be declared before he had made one last effort in favour of peace. Barely had the time allowed come to an end when, on the 1st of Aug. at 2 p. m., he

---

[115] *B. Cor.*, no 138.

[116] No mention is made in the *White Book* of the Russian proposal, amended by England, nor of the Austrian concessions.

addressed the following telegram to the Emperor William: "I can understand that you are obliged to mobilise; but I should like to have from you the same guarantee that I gave you,[117] that these measures do not mean war and that we shall continue our negotiations for the welfare of our respective countries and for general peace, so dear to our hearts. Our long and tried friendship ought, with God's help, to succeed in preventing bloodshed. This is my most earnest desire and I have entire confidence in your reply".[118] This clearly indicated that he remained open to any plan of conciliation. But the same day the Emperor William haughtily rejected this proposal. "An immediate reply", he telegraphed, "clear and unequivocal, from your Government is the only way to avert a most terrible calamity. Until I receive that reply it is impossible for me, to my great regret, to discuss the subject of your telegram". The refusal was brutal.

That very evening, at 7.10, war was officially declared against Russia by Germany. In the note to this effect, which Herr von Pourtalès had caused to be delivered to M. Sazonoff, the only grievance mentioned was the refusal to reply to the German ultimatum.[119] It is curious to note that, when announcing it next day to Sir E. Goschen, Herr von Jagow thought fit to justify it otherwise.[120] Russian troops were said to have crossed the frontier; it would therefore be Russia who, in point of fact had taken the initiative in the war. It goes without saying that this accusation, accompanied by no proof and totally ignored in the official note delivered to M. Sazonoff, was invented from beginning to end. The Austrian Government, however, made use of it when, five days later, it decided at last to follow the example of its ally and to declare war against Russia.[121] It also maintained that Russia had opened hostilities.

---

[117] This guarantee had been given by the Czar in a telegram of the 31st.

[118] *W. B.*, Pref., p. 13.

[119] *O. B.*, no 76.

[120] *B. Cor.*, no 111.

[121] *O. B.*, no 79.

The very diversity of the pretexts alleged suffices to prove that the cause determining war was to be sought elsewhere.

We may wonder how it was that the German Government which on the 29th July had postponed its ultimatum because it feared the intervention of England, three days later took no further account of it. Yet England had not changed her attitude. On the contrary, on the 30th July, Sir E. Grey telegraphed to Sir E. Goschen to confirm him in his opinion that the bargain proposed the day before by the Chancellor in exchange for Great Britain's neutrality, "could not for a moment be entertained. It would be", said he, "a disgrace for us to make this bargain with Germany at the expense of France, a disgrace from which the good name of this country would never recover".[122] On the 1st Aug., when Prince Lichnowsky again endeavoured to obtain formal assurances of neutrality by suggesting "that Germany might guarantee the integrity of France *and her colonies*", Sir E. Grey did not allow himself be tempted by this high bid and maintained his resolution to make no engagement.[123]

His words however were not taken literally. It was not believed that the English Government would recognise that it had at any rate moral obligations, towards France, but it was no doubt thought, that it merely wished to keep its hands free to act according to circumstances. And as Sir E. Grey repeated again and again that his attitude would depend above all on public opinion, an attempt was made to gain the latter. A serious denial of justice, an act of aggression without any apparent reason, might move it. The declaration of war that was contemplated on the 29th July had evidently this character, to declare war against Russia because she had mobilised against Austria, and that when Austria had no fault to find, was to own that war was wanted for war's sake. To break off negotiations in these circumstances was a dangerous game to play. On the other hand, a general mobilisation on the part of Russia

---

[122] *B. Cor.*, no 101.

[123] *B. Cor.*, no 123.

which, with a little skill, might be represented as directed deliberately against Germany, was a more plausible reason and was less likely to upset the pacific sentiments of England. And for this it was better to wait. Patience was all the easier as, from the 30th,[124] it was not difficult to foresee the course that events were about to take, especially if they were helped on a little. The impending general mobilisation of Austria from which Herr von Tschirsky, though no doubt aware of it, did not attempt to dissuade the Austrian Government would necessarily force Russia to a corresponding measure. A better occasion was therefore at hand.

The declaration of war against France. – What was France going to do?

No one doubted that she would fulfil her duty towards her ally. But in order to make it clear to the world that it was Germany's firm resolution to make war against France, the French Government refrained from doing any thing that might resemble an act of hostility. When announcing to our Ambassadors that French mobilisation was ordered, M. Viviani was careful to inform them that it constituted simply a measure of preservation which would not prevent the Government from continuing the negotiations it had already begun.[125] Moreover, to avoid any incident that Germany might be able to interpret as an act of war, the French troops received orders, even after mobilisation, to leave a zone of 10 kilometres between them and the frontier.[126]

But Germany could not wait. The plan of her General Staff was to throw itself immediately on France, to force her to surrender within a few weeks' time and then to turn back against Russia. It was therefore necessary to act swiftly. She waited however as long as she could, probably hoping that

---

[124] On the 30th Herr von Jagow announced that Austria was about to decide on a general mobilisation (*Y. B.*, no 109).

[125] *Y. B.*, no 127.

[126] *Y. B.*, no 136.

France would in the end take the initiative in the rupture and spare her the odium of aggression. But on the 5th Aug. the ultimatum addressed to Belgium expired, hostilities were about to begin, and it was impossible to delay any longer; at 6.45 p. m., Herr von Schoen went to the Quai d'Orsay to ask for his passports and to declare war.

It was not easy to find a reason for a declaration that was not justified by any direct conflict between the two countries. The only allegation made was that French aviators had committed acts of hostility on German territory. One of them was said to have attempted to destroy works near Wesel, others to have been seen over the region of the Eifel, another to have thrown bombs on the railway near Karlsruhe and Nuremberg. The very manner in which these accusations were made suffices to prove that they were trivial and poor inventions. No evidence was brought forward, no details given as to the exact spot where these acts had taken place; nothing was said as to their date, as to the manner in which they had been carried out or as to the nature and extent of the damage caused. All these incidents were presented as though they had happened apart from time and space, which is the best proof of their unreality.[127]

---

[127] As we wished to ascertain whether the German newspapers hqd given a more detailed account of these occurrences, we consulted five of the principal newspapers (*Vorwaerts, Arbiter Zeitung,* of Vienna, *Frankfurter Zeitung, Koelnische Zeitung, Münchner Neueste Nachrichten*) from the end of July to the 5th Aug. First of all we noticed that the aviator who is said to have flown over Karlsruhe is not mentioned. As for the others, the account of them is as vague as it is in the official note. These incidents, given as the cause determining war, take up one line, two or three at the most. *The bombs never left any trace.* One of these aeroplanes, that at Wesel, is said to have been brought down; nothing is said of the aviator and, what became of him, nor is there anything about the aeroplane itself. In a word, the Germans took care to draw attention to their arrival in Germany and then never spoke of them again. They were never seen to return to their starting-point.

But we have still more convincing evidence. We have been able to procure a Nuremberg newspaper, the *Frankischer Kurrier.* On the 2nd Aug., the day the bombs are supposed to have been thrown, not a word is

These inventions were all the more audacious because M. Viviani already on the 2nd Aug. had pointed out to the Government at Berlin distinctly warlike acts which had been committed by German troops on French territory. They had crossed the frontier at Cirey as well as near Longwy; they were marching on the forts bearing the latter name.[128] The customs post at Delle had twice been fired on by a detachment of German soldiers. To the north of this place, two German patrols of the 5th Mounted Chasseurs had advanced as far as the villages of Jonchery and Baron, more than ten kilometres from the frontier. The officer who commanded the former had blown out the brains of a French soldier. The German cavalry had taken away the horses which the Mayor of Suarce was collecting and had forced the inhabitants of the Commune to lead them away.[129] This time the precise details given of the grievances made it possible to verify them.[130] Besides, at the same moment, Luxembourg had already been invaded though: it is true that Herr von Schoen sent M. Viviani a note in which it was said that this invasion, contrary to the international treaties, did not constitute an aggressive action but was merely a preventive measure.[131]

---

said about the incident. Nuremberg received the news on the 3rd by a telegram from Berlin identical to that published by the other newspapers. Again, the *Koelnische Zeitung* of the 3rd Aug. morning edition, published a telegram from Munich which read as follows: "The Bavarian Minister of war is doubtful as to the exactness of the news announcing that aviators had been seen above the lines Nuremberg-Kitzingen and Nuremberg-Ansbach and that they had thrown bombs on the railway."

We have been greatly helped in these researches by our colleague J. Hadamard and M. Edg. Milhaud, professor at the University of Geneva, to whom we tender our sincere thanks.

[128] *Y. B.*, no 136.

[129] *Y. B.*, no 139.

[130] The Chancellor in his speech to the Reichstag on the 4th Aug. maintained that, according to the General Staff, one only of these violations of the frontier had really been committed. Moreover, he tells us neither where nor when it took place.

[131] *Y. B.*, no 136.

For reasons which we shall not seek to determine, Austria-Hungary did not feel called upon to proceed in the same way as her ally: she did not declare war against France. The result was paradoxical: the Austrian Ambassador remained our guest whilst Austrian troops were on our frontier. On the 10th Aug. the French Government put an end to this paradox by recalling M. Dumaine; Herr von Sczesen then asked for his passports.

But there was one member of the Triple Alliance who refused to side with Germany; this was Italy. From the beginning she had disapproved of the Austrian ultimatum. During the negotiations she had supported the efforts of the Triple Entente in favour of peace. In fact on the 1st of Aug. the Marquis di San Giuliano had warned the German Ambassador at Rome that "*the war undertaken . . . having an aggressive character*, and not being in accordance with the purely defensive character of the Triple Alliance, Italy could not take part in the war".[132]

[132] *Y. B.*, no 124. Since writing these lines, we have learnt from a recent speech of Mr Giolitti that already in 1913 Austria wished to bring about a war against Servia and that Italy had refused her cooperation in such an aggression. The Serajevo assassination was therefore merely a pretext.

V. — Conclusion.

These facts being established, the question which forms the title of our book is answered. The facts speak for themselves; they clearly indicate *who wanted war.*

It was evidently not France. Even her worst enemies have not brought such an accusation against her. In fact, she strained every effort and until the last struggled for peace.

It has been said,[133] it is true, that she had never forgotten Alsace-Lorraine. But who would call it a crime in her to be faithful to the religion of remembrance? Such natural and legitimate sentiments could only be made a reproach to her had they revealed themselves by either aggressive or imprudent acts, of a nature to trouble the peace of Europe. But the outward attitude of France was always irreproachably correct. This was distinctly seen at the time of the painful incidents of Saverne.

It would also be as impossible to blame England. It was she who presided at all the attempts at conciliation; it was even she who most often renewed them. England's desire for peace was such that Sir E. Grey would not have hesitated to consider himself free from all obligation towards France and Russia had war broken out through the fault of these two countries. On the 31st July, he telegraphed to Sir E. Goschen: "I said to the German Ambassador this morning that if Germany could get any reasonable proposal put forward which made it clear that German and Austria were striving to preserve European peace, and that Russia and France would be unreasonable if they rejected it, I would support it at St. Petersburg and Paris, and *go the length of saying that if Russia and France would not*

---

133 This was said by the German Chancellor to the Reichstag on the 2nd Dec. 1914.

accept it His Majesty's Government would have nothing more to do with the consequences".[134]

In the preface to the *White Book* the German Government recognised these pacific intentions of England. Since then, it is true, it has changed its mind. To-day the current opinion in Germany is that the responsibility of the war devolves on England. She is accused of having drawn Germany "into an ambuscade",[135] by unmasking her intentions at the eleventh hour; that is equivalent, said the Chancellor, to striking from behind a man who is fighting for his life against two assailants".[136] But these violent protestations simply mean that the German Government did not expect to see England give her support to an invaded Belgium. Herr von Bethmann-Hollweg had been so lavish in offers and in making advances, he had taken so much trouble, especially from the 29th, to appear to be on good terms with England; he had so often assured her of his pacific sentiments, that he believed himself sure of British neutrality. Even in the note in which Germany declared war against Russia, this supposed understanding was mentioned; we find it said there that the Emperor William had undertaken to perform the office of mediator "in agreement with England". Therefore the surprise and disappointment of the Chancellor were great, so great even that they were expressed ingenuously in words which will remain historical.

And yet he had only himself to blame for he had been duly warned. More than once Sir E. Grey had repeated that, if the war became general, he might be obliged to intervene, in particular that, if Germany violated the neutrality of Belgium, "it would be extremely difficult to restrain public feeling in England". He had called the attention of the German Government to the "very serious" nature of the warning he had given it; and meeting in anticipation the reproaches that are ad-

---

134 *B. Cor.*, no 111.

135 The expression was used in the manifesto published by the 93 intellectuals.

136 *B. Cor.*, no 160.

dressed to him to-day, he had added that, after such clear explanations, he could not be accused in the future of having deceived Germany by using equivocal language.[137] Unfortunately German diplomacy is too often lacking in psychological intuition; it cannot divine what is passing in the souls of individuals and of nations, it cannot comprehend the motives which lead them, especially when those motives are complex and delicate. The result is that it foresees wrongly what their conduct will be. To-day it seeks vengeance in groundless accusations for an error of which it alone is guilty.[138]

The attitude of Russia was not less pacific than that of England and of France. It is true that Russia could not consent to leave Servia to her fate. But with the reserve that she could not allow Servia's rights as a sovereign State nor her territory to be impaired, she showed herself ready to accept any transaction. She admitted that guarantees could be asked of the Servian Government, which, moreover did not refuse them. She even went so far in urging moderation as to refrain from taking any grave decision even after Austria had declared war against Servia. She joined in all attempts at conciliation, she proposed several herself, declaring beforehand that she would concur in any that should seem equitable to England and France. "I shall negotiate to the very end", said M. Sazonoff one day, and he kept his word. Germany, it is true, has accused him of having decreed a general mobilisation on the 31st, and on account of this single act she has wished to make the Russian

---

137 *B. Cor.*, nos 123 and 101.

138 We say nothing about another accusation made against England by Herr von Bethmann-Hollweg, namely that it is on her that the *hidden* responsibility of the war will fall because she could have prevented it by letting it be known directly in St. Petersburg "that she would not allow the conflict to take the proportions of a European war." In other words to assure peace England had only to contest Russia's right to intervene, that is to adopt Germany's point of view which she considered unjustifiable. These words of the Chancellor are extraordinarily wanting in perception. Besides, how could England have forced Russia to abstain if the latter refused to yield to her injunction? Would it have been by seeking an alliance with Germany?

Government responsible for the war. She wilfully forgot that such a measure had been imposed on Russia by a similar measure that had already been taken by Austria. Russia could not content herself with opposing the few army corps she was mobilising against the millions of men that Austria was preparing for battle. Besides, we know that M. Sazonoff offered to stop these preparations if Austria would pledge herself to do the same, and it is not Russia's fault if her proposal was disregarded. None of the Powers of the Triple Entente can therefore be incriminated.

How heavy, on the contrary, is the responsibility of Austria! It was she who brought about the cataclysm by addressing an ultimatum to Servia, intentionally unacceptable. Then, when the crisis took place, she forced it towards a violent issue by turning long a deaf ear to any proposed compromise. However we must note in her favour that, if she certainly desired war with Servia, still she did not seem to have sought a general conflagration. If for a while she showed herself unbending, it was with the conviction, carefully maintained by Herr von Tschirsky, that Russia would stand aside, as she had in 1909 after the annexation of Herzegovina and Bosnia. However, when she discovered that she was mistaken and that Russia took the matter seriously, she at once changed her attitude. When Russia mobilised she became conciliatory. On the 29th partial mobilisation was decreed; on the 30th Count Berchtold modified his tone. The more the European war seemed to threaten, the more the Government at Vienna became pacific. When at last it realised what a terrible game it was playing, it tried to draw back. But it was too late. Germany had taken the reins into her own hands and carried Austria along with her. Austria was the victim of the bluff to which she had too easily lent herself. Germany, too, did not speak the truth when she pretended that the military preparations of Russia had prevented her from acting to any purpose at Vienna. It was, on the contrary, at this very moment that Austria grew wiser and herself offered to mediate.[139]

But whatever decreases the responsibility of Austria, increases all the more that of Germany.

It was Germany who, by promising her ally, whose designs she knew, her entire support, encouraged that ally to provoke Servia. It was she who, by approving unreservedly that provocatory attitude, urged Austria to persist in it.

When Russia, England, France and Italy asked that at least a short respite might be granted them to be able to deliberate on the question at issue, hoping tacitly that time and reflexion might exercise a soothing influence, it was Germany who, by refusing to join the other Powers, prevented the request from having any result.

It was she who, whilst professing pacific sentiments, rendered nugatory the plan of Conference of the four Powers, yet proposed nothing that might take its place.

It was she who, when informed of the proposal for direct conversations between Russia and Vienna, to which she could have no objection as it bound her in no way, refused to support

---

[139] Another explanation of the facts is, however possible. It may be wondered if the concessions made by Austria at the eleventh hour, were not a manœuvre in conjunction with Germany. In effect they permitted the latter to maintain that through her influence Austria had become conciliatory, that, consequently peace was assured at the very moment that it was compromised by the sudden mobilisation of Russia.

This interpretation is not absolutely improbable. If we have left it on one side it is because such a manœuvre would have been singularly coarse and unskilful. It did in fact turn against Germany. It made it possible to say, as we have done, that Austria having gone over to the side of peace, this would have been assured, but for the final unbending attitude of Germany. However, the proceedings of the German diplomacy are sometimes so clumsy that the hypothesis cannot be considered as absolutely inadmissible. But were it true, though adding to the responsibility of Austria, it would also only increase that of Germany. What is more ignoble than this Machiavelism which would have consisted in sharing the roles of this most sinister comedy and of obliging Austria to pursue a course of lies so that she and her ally might attain more easily, the abominable aim they were pursuing?

it at Vienna, contenting herself with transmitting it, not without evident ill-will.

It was she who showed herself absolutely aggressive by threatening, from the 29th July, to throw herself upon Russia, though she recognised afterwards that the pretext she had given for doing so was untenable.

It was she who, on the 30th, without consulting Austria, rejected a fresh proposal made by M. Sazonoff which could, at least, have served as a basis for eventual negotiations.

It was she who, when a general mobilisation was decreed everywhere, when war seemed imminent, refused even to look into another proposal for compromise, which might have put off the danger, a proposal that Austria accepted, that all the Powers recommended and which ought to have given entire satisfaction to herself.

Finally it was she who declared war against Russia and against France, justifying this double declaration by lying inventions.

In answer to the concurrent weight of the overwhelming charges, Germany puts forward a case the official version of which is found in the Preface to the *White Book;* its object is to throw the whole of the responsibility upon Russia. It will not take long to discuss this case; it crumbles away as soon as we are acquainted with the method to which it owes its construction.

The author of this preface does not falsify, in the literal sense of the word, the facts he makes use of; *he makes methodical omissions.* Indeed, we find in his account assertions without proofs, others that are manifestly contrary to the truth; we have quoted several of them. Very often events are not dated and the order in which they are given is in no way chronological; there results from this a confusion which renders verification difficult. But after all, though these mistakes and inexactitudes indicate a somewhat indifferent regard for truth, still they are not essential. But though the facts are not outrageously altered, all that contradict the German thesis are carefully passed over in silence, or else they take up so little room in the account that one barely notices them. To prove this, is only necessary to refer to the notes at the foot of the preceding pages: we have pointed out these too clever lapses of memory. We know how many were the attempts at conciliation to which Germany refused her aid. Now in the *White Book* one document alone mentions a refusal of this kind (no 12). The reader who possessed no other source of information would be ignorant of the steps taken by Russia, England and France to obtain an extension of the time-limit of the Austrian ultimatum and of the proposal of direct conversations between Vienna and St. Petersburg.[140] Barely a line or two is devoted to the proposal for a conference of the four Powers to which the Cabinets paid so much attention. Nor is anything said about the efforts made to urge Germany to state in what way she understood the mediation of the Powers, nor about the first German ultimatum, nor about the general mobilisation of Austria and its being anterior to that of Russia, nor about the compromise finally accepted by Austria and rejected by Germany alone. Two groups of facts alone are given and explained in detail; first, some documents in which the German Government expresses, in very general terms, its desire for peace; then, all that bears on the military preparations of France and of Russia, and above all on the general mobilisation of the latter Power, but without giving any explanation of the causes which determined it. The very natural result is that it seems to have taken place quite suddenly, without any kind of justification, at the very moment when the Emperor William was condescending to play the part of mediator. Represented in this light, that mobilisation appears an act of perfidy. To re-establish the truth it is only necessary to re-establish the facts systematically omitted. Then the persistence with which Germany set aside, one after the other, all possible means of maintaining peace, stands out clearly proved, and, at the same time Russia's act loses the aggressive character that it had been desired to impute to it and becomes a simple measure of self-defence.

---

140 In the collection of documents there are two lines on this question (no 15).

To sum up, there does not stand to the credit of Germany a single serious effort in favour of peace; there is nothing but words. On the contrary, all the acts which gradually turned the crisis towards war — the Austrian note, the refusal to prolong the time limit, the declaration of war against Servia, the rejection of the proposed compromises, the first demand to Russia, the ultimatum followed by the declaration of war — all this was either directly desired by her or done with her support and complicity. At the beginning she was behind Austria, whose aggressive policy she supported; then, when once she took matters into her own hands, it was she who took the supreme decisions and impose them on her ally, who was then hesitating and troubled. She therefore is the guilty one.

It has been objected that the Emperor William had shown by acts at different times his desire for peace; his past, it is said, will not allow us to ascribe to him bellicose intentions which his whole character belies. But this would be forgetting that men change with age and with circumstances. In fact there are grounds for believing that William II had changed, that towards the end of 1913, the former champion of peace had begun to incline towards ideas of war. A conversation he had with the king of Belgium in the presence of General von Moltke leaves this impression; M. Cambon, who says he had it from an absolutely reliable source, repeats it in one of the documents in the *Yellow Book* (no 6). The Emperor is represented as having said that he had "come to think that war with France was inevitable and that it must come sooner or later", and General von Moltke is said to have spoken in the same terms.

Very different causes may have determined this moral revolution. The check of the imperial policy in Morocco, the unpopularity which resulted from it, the increasing popularity of the Crown Prince, this all must have made William feel the necessity of raising his prestige by some bold stroke. On the other hand the nationalist agitation in France had been cleverly made use of by the always powerful military party; it was said that France wanted and was preparing her revenge. Finally, the Austro-Hungarian Empire was threatened with disintegration at the death of Francis Joseph; if, therefore, Germany waited too long to act, it was to be feared that, at the important moment, she might find herself without an ally or with an ally weakened and entirely taken up with internal troubles. These general tendencies already very dangerous in themselves, became still more pronounced in July 1914, in consequence of a number of special circumstances. The Archduke Francis Ferdinand was a personal friend of William, besides being a future sovereign. For this double reason the Kaiser felt himself especially called upon to avenge the Serajevo assassination. As, at the same time, England seemed threatened by a kind of civil war, Russia paralysed by very serious strikes, France by intestinal divisions, the occasion was propitious, and it might seem wise not to let it escape.

Besides, the question is not whether William II was or was not a man to wish for war, but whether he and his Government did in fact wish for it. We have seen how facts answer this question. If, nevertheless, the German thesis on the causes of the war could obtain temporary credence, not only in Germany, but in a certain number of neutral countries, it was because the process by which it had been established could not immediately be seen through. The intentional omissions so numerous and so serious, which made it seem plausible, could not be revealed until it was possible to give a systematic account of the origin of the war. But now that we know in what order the events were linked together and what was at each phase of the negotiations the attitude of the different States that took part in them, the guilt of Germany stands out in strong relief. Everything proves it and nothing either weakens or attenuates it. Thus universal opinion hesitates less and less to ascribe to the German Government the responsibility for the terrible calamity which is causing so much suffering to all nations to-day. The truth is even beginning to filter through that kind of Chinese wall which isolates the German Empire to-day from the rest of the world. There are even now Germans who, although they are but very imperfectly enlightened, are troubled in their conscience and already feel the necessity of refusing to associate themselves with the great, the unpardonable falsehood, the history of which has just been related. No doubt, they are as yet only a little band. But how overwhelming must be the evidence of the facts to convince even these who only through cruel suffering can attain to a realisation of the truth.

Additional Note.

The preceding work was already in the press when the *Norddeutsche Allgemeine Zeitung* of the 21st December published a reply to the *Yellow Book*. It contested certain of the fact that are quoted in our study. We shall speak here only of those contentions which bear on the facts of some importance.

1. The concessions made by Austria as from the 30th July are denied. Unfortunately the reality of these concessions was recognised by the German Government itself. On the 1st Aug., when the English Ambassador pointed out to Herr von Jagow that Austria was now quite disposed to talk with Russia, the Secretary of State replied that this conciliatory disposition was due "to German influence". Whatever may have been the origin of this disposition it therefore certainly existed.

2. A partial denial is given to Mr Cambon's despatch relating the conversation between King Albert and William II. The Emperor is said not to have been present at that interview. General von Moltke alone was present and he did not use the terms attributed to him. In reply to this semi-denial we confine ourselves to affirming that the source from which Mr Cambon had his information is "perfectly reliable".

3. Finally, the German Gazette denies that the Austrian mobilisation took place before the Russian general mobilisation: the first is said to have taken place during the day of the 31st, the second during the night of the 30th-31st. But *a*) no proof of any kind is given in support of this assertion. *b*) M. Palèologue's telegram dated the 31st (*Y. B.*, no 118) says expressly that the Russian general mobilisation was determined by the Austrian general mobilisation. No evidence to the contrary is given in support of this denial. *c*) The writer of the article seems to have forgotten that, according to M. Dumaine (*Y. B.*, no 115) the Austrian general mobilisation took place on the 31st *at one o'clock,* which makes it improbable that it could have been provoked by the Russian mobilisation, if the latter took place during the night of the 30th-31st. *d)* Finally, a confession made by Germany decides the point at issue. We have seen (p. 41) that on the 31st

July, at 2 p. m. (Berlin time), William II sent a telegram to the Czar in which there was no question of a Russian general mobilisation. At that time, then, the Government at Berlin was ignorant of it. To begin with, this ignorance at such an advanced hour of the day is incomprehensible if the Russian decree for mobilisation took place the preceding night. What follows will take away all doubt if any can still remain. After having reproduced the text of the Emperor's telegram, the author of the Preface to the *White Book* (p. 12) adds: "This telegram had not yet arrived at its destination when *the mobilisation of all the Russian forces already ordered this same day (31st July) in the morning* (am Vormittag) was being carried out". *Vormittag* means the morning, and indeed rather the later part of the morning, about 11 o'clock, not the night of the 30th-31st. The German Government therefore has given an answer in advance to its newspaper.

This fact established, we must add that the importance attached by Germany to the question of Russian mobilisation is simply and purely pharisaical. Even had that mobilisation not taken place Germany would have mobilised that day and war would have been the result. We have seen in fact how threatening was Wiliiam II's telegram written at two o'clock in the afternoon, though at that time he was ignorant of the Russian mobilisation. And similarly in the morning, the Chancellor announced to the English Ambassador that "serious measures" were going to be taken against Russia, "perhaps to-day" (*B. Cor.*, no 108, 109). And yet he only knew later that Russia was mobilising (*B. Cor.*, no 112). — They were therefore searching for a pretext; the Russian mobilisation simply strengthened the one they already had in view.

CPSIA information can be obtained at www.ICGtesting.com
Printed in the USA
LVOW13s2012290614

392216LV00001B/79/P

9 781610 271486